MACMILLAN LITERATURE COLLECTIONS

Twentieth-Century Stories

edited by Mark Irvine
with Ceri Jones

Series Editor: Ceri Jones

Published by Macmillan ELT
Between Towns Road, Oxford OX4 3PP
A division of Macmillan Publishers Limited
Companies and representatives throughout the world

ISBN 978–0–2304–0853–1

All additional material written by Mark Irvine and Ceri Jones

First published 2011
Text © Macmillan Publishers Limited 2011
Design and illustration © Macmillan Publishers Limited 2011
This version first published 2011

The authors and publishers would like to thank the following for permission
to reproduce the following copyright material: David Higham Associates for
the short story 'Lamb to the Slaughter' by Roald Dahl, published in *Someone
Like You*, 1970, reproduced by permission of David Higham Associates;
Johnson & Alcock Ltd for the short story 'The Teddy-bears' Picnic' by
William Trevor, copyright © William Trevor, *Beyond The Pale*, 1998.
Reproduced with permission of Johnson & Alcock Ltd.; Bloomsbury and
Random House, Inc. for the short story 'The Rich Brother' by Tobias Wolff,
published in *Our Story Begins*, 2008, copyright © 2008 by Tobias Wolff.
Used by permission of Bloomsbury and Alfred A. Knopf, a division of
Random House, Inc; Darhansoff, Verrill, Feldman Literary Agents and
Simon & Schuster, Inc. for 'The Blood Bay,' from *Close Range: Wyoming
Stories* by Annie Proulx, copyright © 1999 by Dead Line, Ltd. All rights
reserved. Used courtesy of Darhansoff, Verrill, Feldman Literary Agents;
and Scribner, a Division of Simon & Schuster, Inc.

Every effort has been made to trace the copyright holders, but if any have
been inadvertently overlooked, the publishers will be pleased to make the
necessary arrangements at the first opportunity.

These materials may contain links for third party websites. We have no
control over, and are not responsible for, the contents of such third party
websites. Please use care when accessing them.

Cover by Skyscan/Underwood & Underwood

Printed and bound in Thailand

2017 2016 2015 2014 2013 2012 2011
10   9   8   7   6   5   4   3   2

Contents

Macmillan Literature Collections

Welcome to the *Macmillan Literature Collections* – a series of advanced-level readers containing original, unsimplified short stories written by famous classic and modern writers. We hope that these stories will help to ease the transition from graded readers to reading authentic novels.

Each collection in the series includes:

Introduction

- an introduction to the short story
- tips for reading authentic texts in English
- an introduction to the genre
- a carefully-chosen selection of classic and modern short stories.

The stories

Each story is presented in three parts: the introduction and pre-reading support material; the story; and post-reading activities. Each part includes the following sections:

- *About the author* – in-depth information about the author and their work
- *About the story* – information about the story, including background information about setting and cultural references
- *Summary* – a brief summary of the story that does not give away the ending.

Pre-reading activities

- *Key vocabulary* – a chance to look at some of the more difficult vocabulary related to the main themes and style of the story before reading the story
- *Main themes* – a brief discussion of the main themes, with questions to keep in mind as you read.

The story

You will find numbered footnotes in the stories. These explain cultural and historical references, and key words that you will need to understand the text. Many of these footnotes give definitions of words which are very formal, old-fashioned or rarely used in modern English. You will find more common, useful words and phrases from the stories in the *Glossary* at the end of the book. Words included in the *Glossary* will appear in **bold**.

Post-reading activities

- *Understanding the story* – comprehension questions that will help you make sure you've understood the story
- *Language study* – a section that presents and practises key linguistic and structural features of authentic literary texts (you will find an index of the areas covered at the end of the book)
- *Literary analysis* – discussion questions that guide you to an in-depth appreciation of the story, its structure, its characters and its style.

In addition, at the end of each book there are:
- suggested *Essay questions*
- a comprehensive *Glossary* highlighting useful vocabulary from each story
- an index for the *Language study* section.

How to use these books

You can use these books in whatever way you want. You may want to start from the beginning and work your way through. You may want to pick and choose. The *Contents* page gives a very brief, one-line introduction to each story to help you decide where to start. You may want to learn about the author and the story before you read each one, or you may prefer to read the story first and then find out more about it afterwards. Remember that the stories and exercises can be challenging, so you may want to spend quite a long time studying each one. The most important thing is to enjoy the collection – to enjoy reading, to enjoy the stories and to enjoy the language that has been used to create them.

Answer keys

In many cases you can check your answers in the story by using the page references given. However, an Answer key for all the exercises is available at www.macmillanenglish.com/readers.

Introduction

What is a short story?

A short story is shorter than a novel, but longer than a poem. It is usually between 1,000 and 20,000 words long. It tells a story which can usually be read quite quickly. It often concentrates on one, central event; it has a limited number of characters, and takes place within a short space of time.

History of the short story

Stories and storytelling have existed for as long as people have had language. People love, and need, stories. They help us explain and understand the world. Before people could read or write, storytellers travelled from village to village, telling stories.

The first written stories developed from this storytelling tradition. Two of the best-known examples of early, written stories in Europe appeared in the 14th century. Chaucer's *Canterbury Tales* and Bocaccio's *Decameron* are both based on the same idea – a group of people who are travelling or living together for a short space of time agree to tell each other stories. Their individual short stories are presented together as one long story.

The first modern short stories appeared at the beginning of the 19th century. Early examples of short story collections include the *Fairy Tales* (1824–26) of the Brothers Grimm, and Edgar Allan Poe's *Tales of the Grotesque and Arabesque* (1840). In the late 19th century, printed magazines and journals became more popular and more and more short stories were published. Nineteenth-century short stories often reflected the literary interest of the time in realism, in stories based on contemporary situations that explored the reality of life at all levels of society.

Short stories in the twentieth century

By the 20th century most well-known magazines included short stories in every issue and the publishers paid a lot of money for them. In 1952, Ernest Hemingway's short story *The Old Man and the Sea* helped sell over five million copies of the magazine *Life* in just over two days. In the first half of the 20th century, some writers managed to make a good living solely out of writing short stories. Later in the same century, short stories became the starting point for novels, or the basis of successful films.

Short stories throughout the 20th century reflected a growing interest in psychology and the inner thoughts and feelings of their characters, echoing literary trends in novels of the same era. As the century progressed, writers also became interested in people's reactions to science and technology and to modern, urban settings. Plots and narratives became less linear. Novels and stories often had open or ambiguous endings, asking questions rather than offering answers, and the reader had to form their own interpretation of facts and motives. Beliefs and social structures were often questioned as the emphasis shifted to the individual and the individual's actions, reactions and thought processes.

The short story today

Today, short stories are often published in collections called anthologies. They are usually grouped according to a particular category – by theme, topic, national origin, time, or author. Some newspapers and magazines continue to print individual stories. Many short stories are first published on the Internet, with authors posting them on special-interest websites and in online magazines.

Reading authentic literary texts in English

Reading authentic literary texts can be difficult. They may contain grammatical structures you have not studied, or expressions and sayings you are not familiar with. Unlike graded readers, they have not been written for language students. The words have been chosen to create a particular effect, not because they are easy or difficult. But you do not need to understand every word to understand and enjoy the story.

When you are reading in your own language you will often read so quickly that you skip over words, and read for the general effect, rather than the details. Try to do the same when you are reading in English. Remember that looking up every word you don't know slows you down and stops you enjoying the story.

When you're reading authentic short stories, remember:
- It should be a pleasure!
- You should read at your own pace.
- Let the story carry you along – don't worry about looking up every word you don't understand.
- Don't worry about looking up difficult words unless they stop you from understanding the story.
- Try not to use the *Glossary* or a dictionary when you're reading.

You might want to make a note of words to look up later, especially key words that you see several times (see *Using a dictionary* on page 10 for more tips on looking up and recording new words). But remember, you can always go back again when you have finished the story. That is the beauty of reading short stories – they are short! You can finish one quite quickly, especially if you do not worry about understanding every single word; then you can start again at the beginning and take your time to re-read difficult passages and look up key words.

Preparing yourself for a story

It is always a good idea to prepare yourself, mentally, before starting a story.
- Look at the title. What does it tell you about the story? What do you expect the story to be about?
- If there is a summary, read it. This will help you follow the story.
- Quickly read the first few paragraphs and answer these questions:
  Where is it set?
  When is it set?
  Who is the main character?
- As you read, concentrate on following the gist (the general idea) of the story. You can go back and look at the details later. You can use the questions at the end of the story (see *Understanding the story*) to help you understand what is happening.

Tips for dealing with difficult passages

Some stories include particularly difficult passages. They are usually descriptive and give background information, or set the scene. They are generally difficult to follow because they are full of detail. Try to read these passages quickly, understanding what you can, and then continue with the story. Make a note of the passage and come back to it later, when you have finished the whole story.

If, at any time, you are finding it difficult to follow the story, go back to this difficult passage. It may hold the answers to your questions.

Read through the passage again carefully and underline all the unknown words. Try to understand as much as you can from the immediate context and what you now know about the story. Then, look up any remaining words in the *Glossary* at the back of the book, or in your dictionary.

Tips for dealing with difficult words

- Decide if the word (or phrase) is important to the overall message. Read the whole paragraph. Do you understand the general meaning? Yes? Then the word isn't important. Don't worry about it. *Keep reading!*
- If you decide the word is important, see if you can work out its meaning from the context. Is it a verb, a noun or an adjective? Is it positive or negative? How would you translate it in your own language? Underline the word or make a note of it and the page number, but *keep reading*. If it really is important, you'll see it again.
- If you keep seeing the same word in the story, and you still can't understand it, look in your monolingual dictionary!

Using a dictionary

Looking up words

Before you look up the word, look at it again in its context. Decide what part of speech it is. Try to guess its meaning from the context. Now look it up in your dictionary. There may be more than one definition given. Decide which one is the most appropriate. If the word is something very specific, e.g. the name of a flower or tree, you can use a bilingual dictionary to give you the exact translation.

Let's look at how this works in practice. Look at this short extract and follow the instructions below.

> …there is a little valley or rather **lap** of land among high hills, which is one of the quietest places in the whole world. A small **brook** glides through it, with just murmur enough to **lull** one to repose*
>
> *literary: sleep or rest*
> *The Legend of Sleepy Hollow* by Washington Irvine

1 Look at the words in bold and decide what part of speech they are – noun, verb, adjective, etc.
2 Try to guess what they might mean.
3 Look at the extracts below from the *Macmillan English Dictionary for Advanced Learners*. Choose the most appropriate definition.

Words with more than one entry	
Sometimes the same word belongs to more than one word class: for example, *brook* can be both a noun and a verb. Each word class is shown as a separate entry. The small number at the end of the head-word tells you that a word has more than one entry.	**brook¹** noun a small river **brook²** verb **not brook** – to definitely not allow or accept something **lap¹** noun **1** the top half of your legs above your knees when you sit down **2** one complete turn around a course in a race PHRASE **in the lap of luxury** in very comfortable and expensive conditions **lap²** verb if an animal laps water, it drinks it gently with its tongue **lull¹** noun a quiet period during a very active or violent situation
Idioms and fixed expressions Some words are often used in idioms and fixed expressions. These are shown at the end of the entry, following the small box that says PHRASE.	
Words with more than one meaning Many words have more than one meaning, and each different meaning is shown by a number.	**lull²** verb **1** to make someone feel relaxed and confident so that they are not prepared for something unpleasant to happen *to lull someone into a false sense of security* **2** to make someone relaxed enough to go to sleep

Dictionary extracts adapted from the *Macmillan English Dictionary* © Macmillan Publishers Limited 2005
www.macmillandictionary.com

Keeping a record

When you have looked in your dictionary, decide if the word is interesting or useful to you. If it is, make a note of it, and write down its definition. Make a note of the sentence where you found it in the story, then write one or two more examples of your own. Only do this for those words you think you will need to use in the future.

Here is an example of how you might record the word *lull*.

> 'with just murmur enough to lull one to repose'
> Lull – to make you feel relaxed enough to go to sleep
> e.g. The quiet sound of the waves lulled me to sleep.
> The mother sang to her baby to lull it to sleep.

Literary analysis

The *Literary analysis* section is written to encourage you to consider the stories in more depth. This will help you to appreciate them better and develop your analytical skills. This section is particularly useful for those students who are studying, or intending to study, literature in the medium of English. Each section includes literary terms with which you may or may not be familiar.

Macmillan Readers website

For more help with understanding these literary terms, and to find Answer keys to all the exercises and activities, visit the Macmillan Readers website at www.macmillanenglish.com/readers. There you will also find a wealth of resources to help your language learning in English, from listening exercises to articles on academic and creative writing.

A Lesson on a Tortoise

by D H Lawrence

About the author

David Herbert Lawrence (1885–1930) was the youngest son of five children. He was born in the mining village of Eastwood, near the city of Nottingham in central England. His father was a coal miner and his mother had been a school teacher before she married. The difference in their backgrounds and education caused a lot of problems in their marriage. Mrs Lawrence was disappointed with her life. She wanted her children's lives to be better – she did not want her daughters to be servants or her sons to become miners. She was therefore very proud when her youngest son, David, won a scholarship to Nottingham High School. Unfortunately, though, David did not do well at school, and when he left in 1901, he worked for a short time as a factory clerk. But he soon became ill and had to give up his job. After a long illness, he became a pupil-teacher[1] at the British School in Eastwood, where he stayed for three years. This time he was more successful, and in 1904, he did outstandingly well in the King's Scholarship exam[2] and went on to study for his teacher's certificate at University College, Nottingham.

Once he had completed his training, he moved to London, where he got a job in a large school in Croydon, South London. In 1909, his first poems were published after Jessie Chambers, a childhood girlfriend who shared his love of books and literature, sent some of his poems to a magazine, the *English Review*[3]. But it was not until after his mother died in December 1910, and after Lawrence himself nearly died a year later of pneumonia, that he felt ready to stop work as a teacher and dedicate himself to writing.

In March 1912, Lawrence fell in love with Frieda von Richthofen, a German aristocrat and wife of his former professor at university. Frieda was six years older than Lawrence and had three young children. Eventually, Lawrence persuaded her to leave her husband and children and they travelled first to Germany, to her hometown of Metz, and

1 someone who is both teaching and studying at the same school
2 an exam for students who could not afford to pay for university fees
3 a literary magazine published in London from 1908 to 1937

then to Italy. It was in Italy that Lawrence, inspired by the beauty of the country and his love for a fiercely independent woman, completed the novel *Sons and Lovers*. Lawrence and Frieda argued passionately. She was, he said, 'the one possible woman for me, for I must have opposition – something to fight'.

Lawrence and Frieda returned to England and married in July 1914. Life in England was difficult for the Lawrences. Many people disapproved of their marriage, and there was a lot of anti-German feeling because of the war. Lawrence continued to write, and to publish, but many people were hostile towards this work – his honest descriptions of love and relationships were considered shocking at the time. His next major novel, *The Rainbow*, was banned and Lawrence longed to escape to America, but the world was at war, and he could not get visas for himself and Frieda.

In 1915, the couple moved to Cornwall, where Lawrence finally finished his novel *Women in Love*, which he had begun writing as a teenager. The couple's lives remained difficult – Lawrence was ill and they had little money, but he continued to earn a living from his writing.

After the war, in 1919, the Lawrences left England for Europe. They lived in Italy, Malta, Austria and Germany. Lawrence continued writing novels, poetry and some non-fiction. He wrote a history book which was used in English schools. However, it had to be published under a pseudonym[4] because of Lawrence's bad reputation. Lawrence returned twice to England for short visits, but he continued to talk about Eastwood as 'the country of my heart'.

In 1922, the Lawrences left Europe and travelled more widely. But ultimately, poor health brought them back to Italy, and they bought a villa near Florence. Here, Lawrence wrote his last major novel, *Lady Chatterley's Lover*, about an aristocratic woman who falls in love with a gamekeeper[5]. The novel was published in Italy, but was banned in a high-profile court case in the UK. His health worsened and on 2nd March 1930, Lawrence died from tuberculosis in Vence, France. He was 44 years old.

Lawrence was an unconventional man in his lifestyle and his writings. On the whole, his work was not understood or fully appreciated in his lifetime. After his death, Lawrence's reputation continued to

4 a false name used by a writer
5 a person who looks after the animals used for hunting of a large house or estate

grow. Several of his novels became very well known, particularly *Sons and Lovers*, *Women in Love*, *The Rainbow* and *Lady Chatterley's Lover*.

Lawrence's background and experiences growing up in a mining village led to his beliefs that increasing industrialization degraded people and caused workers to live a life of ugliness. He believed that people needed beauty to live, and he was extremely sensitive to all forms of beauty in nature. His best work reveals his love of life and living things, and his detailed examination of the relationship between men and women.

About the story

A Lesson on a Tortoise was written in 1908 or 1909, when Lawrence was working as a teacher in a large school in London. It is closely based on his experiences there. It was not published during his lifetime. In 1973 it was included in a collection of the best of *Lawrence on Education* (Penguin).

Background information

Elementary education

In 1870 Parliament introduced compulsory education for all children aged 5–13. The education provided was to be affordable and acceptable to different religious interests. Emphasis was on reading, writing and arithmetic[6]. It also aimed to teach values, such as respect for a teacher's authority and the need for punctuality, obedience and conformity. It was based on a 'monitorial system', where a teacher supervised a large class with assistance from a team of monitors – or helpers – who were usually older students.

Lawrence's experience as a teacher

When Lawrence first started teaching in Croydon, in South London, he described himself in a letter to a friend as: 'a quivering[7] greyhound set to mind[8] a herd of pigs.' After a month he wrote to another friend: 'It is the cruellest and most humiliating sport, this of teaching and trying to tame some fifty or sixty malicious young human animals.'

6 the part of mathematics that involves basic calculations such as adding or
   multiplying numbers
7 trembling
8 look after

But soon he was in control of the situation and able to write: 'School is really very pleasant here. I have tamed my wild beasts – I have conquered my turbulent subjects[9], and can teach in ease and comfort.'

Summary

It may help you to know something about what happens in the story before you read it. Don't worry, this summary does *not* tell you how the story ends!

The storyteller is a teacher of a difficult class of 11-year-old boys in a state school in London. It is the last lesson of the week, on Friday afternoon, and the subject is Nature Study. The teacher has brought in a live tortoise for the boys to sketch[10], and he hopes that the class will enjoy doing something new and special.

The lesson starts well. The boys are excited but able to concentrate and work hard. The teacher enjoys looking out of the window at a beautiful sunset. But then one boy asks if they can have rubbers. The teacher had previously refused to let them use rubbers because too many had disappeared in recent weeks. After the teacher says yes, it becomes apparent that another four rubbers have gone missing. The teacher gets angry and decides he must find out who is responsible.

9 people who live under the control of a king or queen
10 draw a picture quickly and with few details

Pre-reading activities

Key vocabulary

This section will help you familiarize yourself with some of the more specific vocabulary used in the story. You may want to use it to help you before you start reading, or as a revision exercise after you have finished the story.

Describing the tortoise and the boys

1 Look at the words in bold. They are used to talk about parts of the tortoise. Complete the definitions using the words in the box.

| feet   chest   body   toes |

---

ribs long, curved bones that are in the .... of an animal
paws the .... of some animals such as cats or dogs
claws the sharp curved parts at the end of some animals' ...., such as a cat or dog
shell the hard outer part that protects the .... of some animals, such as crabs or snails

---

2 Look at the adjectives and their definitions. For each adjective, decide whether it describes the tortoise, the boys or both.

---

bony so thin that the shape of the bones can be seen
bright intelligent
coarsely dressed wearing poor clothes
crop haired with very short hair
horny hard and rough
lively full of energy

Movement

3 Verbs of movement are important in creating the mood of the story. Look at these short extracts and match the verbs in bold with their definitions (a–g) below.

1 *When I came back I found Joe…**stretching** slowly his skinny neck.*
2 *I **crouched** to look at Joe, and **stroked** his horny, blunt head.*
3 *He **spread out** his legs and **gripped** the floor.*
4 *The boy **dragged himself** to the front of the class.*
5 *Joe **sunk**, and lay flat on his shell, his legs limp.*

a) to move your body close to the ground by bending your knees and leaning forward slightly

b) to move slowly as if your body was very heavy

c) to hold something tightly

d) to move your arms, hand or legs so that they are far apart

e) to make a part of your body as long as possible, often in order to reach something

f) to gently move your hand across skin, hair or fur

g) to fall, sit or lie down

4 Look again at the extracts in exercise 3. Which do you think are describing: a) the tortoise's movements; b) one of the boys' movements?

Key phrasal verbs

5 The following phrasal verbs are all key to the action and interaction in the story. Match the verbs in bold in the sentences below with their definitions (a–g).

1 I don't know why he always **picks on** me – I've never done anything to hurt him!

2 The police **let** him **off** with a warning not to do it again.

3 Both leaders feared that the other would **go back on** his word.

4 I had been trying to get through to him on the phone all day, but in the end I just had to **give up**.

5 If you **keep up** your good work, you'll do well in your final exam.

6 It was easy to **pick out** his son from the group of children playing in the playground – they looked so alike.

7 Eventually he **owned up** to having kicked the football at his neighbour's window.

a) to stop doing something because you are not succeeding

b) to fail to do something that you have agreed or promised to do

c) to continue to do something

d) to give someone little or no punishment for doing something wrong

e) to confess to something

f) to keep treating someone badly or unfairly

g) to recognize someone or something from a group

Once you have read the story, look back and notice how these phrasal verbs were used, and what they were describing.

Non-standard English

There are a few examples of non-standard vocabulary, grammar and pronunciation in the story.

6 **Look at the following extracts from the text, in which the orphan boys from Gordon Home speak about the missing rubbers. Match the examples of non-standard English (a–h) in the excerpts with the descriptions (1–6) below. Note: Some of the descriptions have more than one answer.**

I don't know where they are – I've never (a) 'ad (b) no rubbers.
You pick on us…you pick on Marples, (c) an' Rawson, an' on me.
That doesn't (d) say (e) as we do now.
I shouldn't (f) 'a done if you hadn't (g) 'a been (h) goin' to cane me.

1 the use of *as* in place of *that*
2 the use of *say* to mean *mean*
3 a double negative
4 the dialect pronunciation of *have* as *a*
5 a dropped consonant at the end of a word
6 a dropped /h/ sound at the beginning of a word

7 **Rewrite the excerpts in exercise 6 in standard English.**

Main themes

Before you read the story, you may want to think about some of its main themes. The questions will help you think about the story as you are reading it for the first time. There is more discussion of the main themes in the *Literary analysis* section after the story.

The natural world

Even though the story takes place in a classroom, the natural world also plays an important role. The teacher hopes that by bringing the natural world into the classroom he can engage and stimulate his students, as well as give them a welcome change from the normal classroom routine. The teacher himself, tired at the end of a long week, is also particularly sensitive to the changes in the natural world outside his window, which shape and reflect his changing mood.

8 **As you read the story think about the description and the importance of:**

a) the tortoise
b) the sunset
c) the night sky

Teaching

Before Lawrence was able to earn enough money from his writing to live on, he worked as a teacher. He was not always happy with the role and often struggled to control both his pupils and his classes. *A Lesson on a Tortoise* can be read partly as an autobiographical account of his own experience.

9 **As you read the story, ask yourself:**

a) What is the teacher's attitude to his class, and to this lesson in particular?
b) What mistakes, if any, does he make?
c) Who is responsible for the mood at the end of the story?

⑳

A Lesson on a Tortoise

by D H Lawrence

It was the last lesson on Friday afternoon, and this, with Standard VI[11], was Nature Study from half past three till half past four. The last lesson of the week is a **weariness** to teachers and scholars. It is the end; there is no need to keep up the tension of discipline and effort any longer, and, **yielding** to weariness, a teacher is spent[12].

But Nature Study is a pleasant lesson. I had got a big old tortoise, who had not yet gone to sleep[13], though November was darkening the early afternoon, and I knew the boys would enjoy sketching him. I put him under the radiator to warm while I went for a large empty shell that I had **sawn** in two to show the ribs of some ancient tortoise absorbed in his bony coat. When I came back I found Joe, the old reptile, stretching slowly his skinny neck, and looking with indifferent eyes at the two **intruding** boys who were kneeling beside him. I was too good-tempered to send them out again into the playground, too **slack** with the great relief of Friday afternoon. So I bade[14] them put out the Nature books ready. I crouched to look at Joe, and stroked his horny, blunt head with my finger. He was quite lively. He spread out his legs and gripped the floor with his flat hand-like paws, then he slackened again as if from a yawn, **drooping** his head meditatively.

I felt pleased with myself, knowing that the boys would be delighted with the lesson. 'He will not want to walk,' I said to myself, 'and if he takes a sleepy **stride**, they'll be just in

---

11 school years at the time were called Standard I, II, III and so on. Standard I was the first year of primary education, which started at the age of five. Children in Standard VI (six), would have been 10 or 11 years old

12 *literary:* very tired

13 tortoises hibernate, that is to say, they sleep in the winter

14 *literary:* ordered

20 | A Lesson on a Tortoise

ecstasy, and I can easily calm him down to his old position.' So I **anticipated** their entry. At the end of playtime I went to bring them in. They were a small class of about thirty – my own boys. A difficult, mixed class, they were, consisting of six London Home[15] boys, five boys from a fairly **well-to-do** Home for the children of actors[16], and a set of commoners[17] varying from poor **lads** who **hobbled** to school, **crippled** by broken enormous boots, to boys who brought soft, light shoes to wear in school on snowy days. The Gordons[18] were a difficult set; you could pick them out: crop haired, coarsely dressed lads, distrustful, always ready to assume the defensive. They would lie till it made my heart sick if they were charged with offence, but they were willing, and would respond beautifully to an **appeal**. The actors were of different fibre, some gentle, a pleasure even to look at; others polite and obedient, but indifferent, **covertly insolent** and vulgar; all of them more or less gentlemanly.

The boys crowded round the table noisily as soon as they discovered Joe. 'Is he alive? – Look, his head's coming out! He'll bite you? – He *won't!*' – with much **scorn** – 'Please Sir, do tortoises bite?' I hurried them off to their seats in a little group in front, and pulled the table up to the desks. Joe kept fairly still. The boys **nudged** each other excitedly, making half audible remarks concerning the poor reptile, looking quickly from me to Joe and then to their neighbours. I set them sketching, but in their pleasure at the **novelty** they could not be still:

'Please Sir – shall we draw the marks on the shell? Please sir, has he only got four toes?' – 'Toes!' echoes somebody, covertly delighted at the absurdity of calling the grains of claws 'toes'. 'Please Sir, he's moving – Please Sir!'

I stroked his neck and calmed him down:

'Now don't make me wish I hadn't brought him. That's

15 children from a Church of England orphanage called Gordon Home in Croydon, South London. The home was named after General Gordon (1833–85), a British army officer
16 an institution for the orphan, illegitimate and unwanted children of actors and actresses
17 not members of any particular institution
18 see note 15

enough. Miles – you shall go to the back and draw **twigs** if I hear you again! Enough now – be still, get on with the drawing, it's hard!'

I wanted peace for myself. They began to sketch diligently. I stood and looked across at the sunset, which I could see facing me through my window, a great gold sunset, very large and magnificent, rising up in immense gold beauty beyond the town, that was become a low dark **strip** of nothingness under the wonderful upbuilding[19] of the western sky. The light, the thick, heavy golden sunlight which is only seen in its full dripping splendour in town, spread on the desks and the floor like **lacquer**. I lifted my hands, to take the sunlight on them, smiling faintly to myself, trying to shut my fingers over its tangible richness.

'Please Sir!' – I was interrupted – 'Please Sir, can we have rubbers?'

The question was rather **plaintive.** I had said they should have rubbers no more. I could not keep my **stock**, I could not detect the thief among them, and I was weary of the continual **degradation** of bullying them to try to recover what was lost among them. But it was Friday afternoon, very peaceful and happy. Like a bad teacher, I went back on my word.

'Well –!' I said indulgently.

My monitor, a pale, bright, **erratic** boy, went to the cupboard and took out a red box.

'Please Sir!' he cried, then he stopped and counted again in the box. 'Eleven! There's only eleven, Sir, and there were fifteen when I put them away on Wednesday –!'

The class stopped, every face upturned. Joe sunk, and lay flat on his shell, his legs **limp**. Another of the hateful moments had come. The sunset was **smeared** out, the charm of the afternoon was smashed like a fair glass[20] that falls to the floor. My nerves seemed to tighten and to vibrate with sudden tension.

'Again!' I cried, turning to the class in passion, to the upturned faces, and the sixty watchful eyes.

19 *poetic use:* something formed by combining different parts
20 *old fashioned:* a mirror

'Again! I am sick of it, sick of it I am! A thieving, **wretched** set! – a **skulking**, mean lot!' I was quivering with anger and **distress**.

'Who is it? You must know! You are all as bad as one another, you hide it – a miserable –!' I looked round the class in great agitation. The Gordons with their distrustful faces, were noticeable:

'Marples!' I cried to one of them, 'where are those rubbers?'

'I don't know where they are – I've never 'ad no rubbers' – he almost shouted back, with the usual insolence of his set. I was more angry:

'You must know! They're gone – they don't melt into air, they don't fly – who took them then? Rawson, do you know anything of them?'

'No Sir!' he cried, with **impudent** indignation.

'No, you intend to know nothing! Wood, have you any knowledge of these four rubbers?'

'No!' he shouted, with absolute insolence.

'Come here!' I cried, 'come here! Fetch the cane, Burton. We'll make an end, insolence and thieving and all.'

The boy dragged himself to the front of the class, and stood slackly, almost crouching, **glaring** at me. The rest of the Gordons sat upright in their desks, like animals of a **pack** ready to **spring**. There was tense silence for a moment. Burton handed me the cane, and I turned from the class to Wood. I liked him best among the Gordons.

'Now my lad!' I said. 'I'll cane you for impudence first.'

He turned swiftly to me; tears sprang to his eyes.

'Well,' he shouted at me, 'you always pick on the Gordons – you're always on to us –!' This was so manifestly untrue that my anger fell like a bird shot in mid-flight.

'Why!' I exclaimed, 'what a disgraceful untruth[21]! I am always excusing you, letting you off –!'

'But you pick on us – you start on us – you pick on Marples, an' Rawson, an' on me. You always begin with the Gordons.'

21 *formal*: a lie

'Well,' I answered, justifying myself, 'isn't it natural? Haven't you boys stolen – haven't these boys stolen – several times – and been caught?'

'That doesn't say as we do now,' he replied.

'How am I to know? You don't help me. How do I know? Isn't it natural to suspect you –?'

'Well, it's not us. We know who it is. Everybody knows who it is – only they won't tell.'

'Who knows?' I asked.

'Why Rawson, and Maddock, and Newling, and all of 'em.'

I asked these boys if they could tell me. Each one shook his head, and said 'No Sir.' I went round the class. It was the same. They lied to me every one.

'You see,' I said to Wood.

'Well – they won't own up,' he said. 'I shouldn't 'a done if you hadn't 'a been goin' to cane me.'

This frankness was painful, but I preferred it. I made them all sit down. I asked Wood to write his knowledge on a piece of paper, and I promised not to **divulge**. He would not. I asked the boys he had named, all of them. They refused. I asked them again – I appealed to them.

'Let them all do it then!' said Wood. I tore up **scraps** of paper, and gave each boy one.

'Write on it the name of the boy you suspect. He is a thief and a **sneak.** He gives endless pain and trouble to us all. It is your duty.'

They wrote **furtively**, and quickly doubled up the papers. I collected them in the lid of the rubber box, and sat at the table to examine them. There was dead silence, they all watched me. Joe had withdrawn into his shell, forgotten.

A few papers were blank; several had 'I suspect nobody' – these I threw in the paper basket; two had the name of an old thief, and these I tore up; eleven bore the name of my assistant monitor, a splendid, handsome boy, one of the oldest of the actors. I remembered how **deferential** and polite he had been when I had asked him, how ready to make barren suggestions; I remembered his **shifty**, anxious look during the questioning;

I remembered how eager he had been to do things for me before the monitor came in the room. I knew it was he – without remembering:

'Well!' I said, feeling very wretched when I was convinced that the papers were right. 'Go on with the drawing.'

They were very **uneasy** and restless, but quiet. From time to time they watched me. Very shortly, the bell rang. I told the two monitors to collect up the things, and I sent the class home. We did not go into prayers[22]. I, and they, were in no mood for **hymns** and the evening prayer of gratitude.

When the monitors had finished, and I had turned out all the lights but one, I sent home Curwen, and kept my assistant monitor a moment.

'Ségar, do you know anything of my rubbers?'

'No Sir' – he had a deep, manly voice, and he spoke with **earnest** protestation – **flushing**.

'No? Nor my pencils? – nor my two books?'

'No Sir! I know nothing about the books.'

'No? The pencils then –?'

'No Sir! Nothing! I don't know anything about them.'

'Nothing, Ségar?'

'No Sir.'

He hung his head, and looked so humiliated, a fine, handsome lad, that I gave it up. Yet I knew he would be dishonest again, when the opportunity arrived.

'Very well! You will not help as monitor any more. You will not come into the classroom until the class comes in – any more. You understand?'

'Yes Sir' – he was very quiet.

'Go along then.'

He went out, and silently closed the door. I turned out the last light, tried the cupboards, and went home.

I felt very tired, and very sick. The night had come up, the clouds were moving darkly, and the **sordid** streets near the school felt like disease in the lamplight.

22 a religious service held at the end of the day

Post-reading activities

Understanding the story

Use these questions to help you check that you have understood the story.

Before the lesson

1 How does the teacher feel?
2 Who is Joe? Why is he in class?
3 Where does the teacher put Joe before going out of the classroom? Why?
4 Who has come into the classroom in his absence?
5 Did they have permission to come into the classroom?
6 Why doesn't the teacher send them back out?
7 What does he ask them to do?
8 Where are the other students?

The class

9 How many students are there in his class?
10 In what way is it a mixed class?
11 Which group does the teacher think is particularly difficult? Why?
12 Does he enjoy teaching them?

The lesson

13 How do the students react to Joe?
14 How does the teacher calm them down?
15 What does the teacher want? Does he get it?
16 Is he paying attention to his class? Why/Why not?
17 At this point what is the mood in the classroom?

The rubbers

18 Why do the boys want rubbers?
19 What is the teacher's first reaction to their request?
20 Why does he get so angry?
21 Who is he angry with?
22 Are you surprised at his reaction? Are the students surprised?
23 Why does he accuse Marples?
24 How does Marples defend himself?
25 What effect does this have on the teacher?
26 Why does the teacher decide to punish Wood?
27 How does the boy react?
28 How does the teacher justify himself?

29 Whose suggestion is it that all the boys write the name of the thief on pieces of paper?
30 Does the idea work?
31 What do the boys do for the rest of the lesson?
32 What is the mood in the class now?

After the lesson

33 What do they not do that they would normally do at the end of the lesson? Why?
34 How does Ségar feel about being accused?
35 Does he admit to the theft?
36 How does the teacher punish him?
37 What does the teacher do before leaving the classroom?
38 How does the teacher feel as he leaves the classroom?

Language study

Would

The modal auxiliary verb *would* has many functions, some of which can be seen in the story.

1 Look at the list of functions of *would*. Which do you think are present in the story?

1 to talk about an imaginary situation in the present
2 to talk about an imaginary situation in the future
3 to talk about tendencies or habitual actions in the past
4 to talk about the future in the past
5 to talk about a determination to do/not do something in the past

2 Match the bold text in the story extracts below (a–f) with functions from the list in exercise 1.

a) *I knew the boys* **would enjoy** *sketching him.*
b) *I felt pleased with myself, knowing that the boys* **would be** *delighted with the lesson.*
c) *They* **would lie** *till it made my heart sick if they were charged with offence.*
d) *They were willing, and* **would respond** *beautifully to an appeal.*
e) *Yet I knew he* **would be** *dishonest again, when the opportunity arrived.*
f) *I asked Wood to write his knowledge on a piece of paper, and I promised not to divulge. He* **would not**.

3 Rewrite the following sentences using *would*. Then match them with the functions in exercise 1.

1 I knew he was probably going to regret his decision for the rest of his life.
2 She refused to help him with his family commitments.
3 If I was offered a good job, I might move to another country.
4 Even if I had a lot more money, I can't imagine leaving my job.
5 In the evenings we used to sit around the fire and tell stories.

Word formation

The story describes a brief moment which is charged with emotions and shifts in mood. Many abstract adjectives and nouns are used to describe those emotions and the attitudes of the main characters.

4 Look at the list of adjectives on the left below. Who or what in the story does each adjective describe?

Adjectives	Nouns
agitated	agitation
angry	....
frank	frankness
humiliated	....
insolent	insolence
obedient	....
silent	....
slack	slackness
weary	....

5 Complete the second column of the table above with the nouns deriving from the adjectives.

6 Look again at the table in exercise 4. There are four noun endings. What are they? Can you think of any other nouns with these endings? What is the adjective for each of those nouns? Could they be used to describe anyone or anything in the story?

7 Choose the correct form to complete the following extracts.

1 *The last lesson of the week is a **weary/weariness** to teachers and scholars.*
2 *I was too good-tempered to send them out again into the playground, too **slack/slackness** with the great relief of Friday afternoon.*
3 *The actors were of different fibre, some gentle, a pleasure even to look at;*

others polite and **obedient/obedience**, but indifferent, covertly **insolent/insolence** and vulgar.

4 I was quivering with **angry/anger** and distress.
5 I looked round the class in great **agitated/agitation**.
6 This **frank/frankness** was painful.
7 There was dead **silent/silence**, they all watched me.
8 He hung his head, and looked so **humiliated/humiliation**, a fine, handsome lad, that I gave it up.

Adverbs of manner with direct speech

A large part of the action in the story is told through dialogue, and the author often uses adverbs and adverbial phrases to clarify the emotions behind the words.

8 Look at these extracts. Practise reading the direct speech using the appropriate emotion.

a) 'Well –!' I said **indulgently**.
b) 'I've never 'ad no rubbers' – he almost shouted back, **with the usual insolence** of his set.
c) 'Well!' I said, **feeling very wretched**.

9 Look at the extracts in exercise 8 again. Match the adverbials in bold with their type (1–3) below.

1 present participle clauses (-ing verb + object, complement or adverb)
2 prepositional phrases (preposition + noun phrase)
3 -ly adverbs of manner

10 Rewrite the sentences below so that the meaning stays the same.

1 'Please get back to your sketching,' I said quietly.
   'Please get back to your sketching,' I said in .... voice.
   'Please get back to your sketching,' I said, speaking ....
2 'He won't bite you!' he said, with much scorn.
   'He won't bite you!' he said ....ly.
   'He won't bite you!' he said, speaking ....
3 'Again!' I cried, turning to the class in passion.
   'Again!' I cried, ... ly.
   'Again!' I cried, with ....

Literary analysis

Plot

1 Number the main events below in the order in which they happened. Which do you think was the one most important event? Why?
   a) The lesson finished.
   b) The monitor told the teacher there were only eleven rubbers left.
   c) The boys wrote the name of the thief on pieces of paper.
   d) The teacher spoke to the thief.
   e) One of the boys asked for a rubber.
   f) The teacher called one of the boys to the front.
2 Do you think the teacher's reaction was reasonable? Why/Why not? Do you think he handled the situation well? What else could he have done?
3 What do you think will happen in the future? How do you think the teacher will feel teaching the same class on Monday morning?
4 The story is called *A Lesson on a Tortoise*. What lessons were learnt in the story? By whom?

Character

5 How many people are there in the story? How many of them are named? Who are they? What is their role in the story?
6 Who do you think are the three most important characters? Why? What do we learn about these characters? What more would you like to know about them? Which character do you feel you know best? Why?
7 Think of the teacher. What do you know about him? Do you know his name, his age, whether or not he's married, if he has children? Why aren't we told this information?
8 Think of Wood. What do you know about him? In what way might his behaviour be considered unusual? Do you sympathize with him? Why/Why not?
9 What about Ségar – do you think he is guilty? Why/Why not? In your opinion, has the teacher assessed Ségar's character correctly? Has he treated him fairly? What do you think the teacher would have done if Ségar had confessed to the theft? How would this have changed the end of the story?

Narration

10 Who tells the story? How would the story have been different if it had been told from the point of view of:
   a) the boy who asked for a rubber?
   b) the monitor?
   c) Wood?
   d) Ségar?
11 What are the advantages of using a first person narrator? What aspect of the story comes through more strongly because of this choice?

Style

12 Read the first paragraph again. What feeling is emphasized in this paragraph? In what way does it prepare us for the story?
13 In the second paragraph a mood change is signalled by the word *but*. What adjective/s would you use to describe the new mood? Choose three words that sum up the atmosphere. How does the description of the tortoise's behaviour add to the general atmosphere?
14 Look at the description of when the boys enter the classroom and crowd around the tortoise [page 21]. Notice the adverbs that are used to describe the boys' behaviour and how they capture the mood. Notice the use of direct speech. What image do you get of the class?

Similes and imagery

Lawrence's style is very rich in similes and imagery, particularly when he is creating atmosphere, or describing the reactions and moods of his characters.

Similes are used to compare a person or thing with another, using the preposition *like* or *as* and focusing on similarities and characteristics that they have in common:

> The rest of the Gordons sat upright in their desks, **like** animals of a pack ready to spring.

Lawrence is describing the reaction of the boys. He compares them to a pack of animals. By doing this he shows us how the teacher feels about these particular boys (he sees them as a group rather than as individuals) and about his role as a teacher (someone who has to control and tame wild animals).

15 Look at the similes below. What is being described? What is it being compared with? What is the effect created by the comparison?
  a) *The light, the thick, heavy golden sunlight…spread on the desks and the floor like lacquer.*
  b) *The charm of the afternoon was smashed like a fair glass that falls to the floor.*
  c) *My anger fell like a bird shot in mid-flight.*
  d) *The sordid streets near the school felt like disease in the lamplight.*

  Which of the similes is your favourite? Why?

We use the term **imagery** to talk about the specific words and phrases used in a description to create an image of something.

16 Look at the following description from the story. Notice the imagery that is used in describing the sunset. Which adjective is repeated? What associations does this word have? How does this add to the description? What other adjectives are used to describe the sunset? Compare them to the adjectives and imagery used to describe the town. What does this tell us about the teacher's frame of mind[23]?

  I could see facing me through my window, a great gold sunset, very large and magnificent, rising up in immense gold beauty beyond the town, that was become a low, dark strip of nothingness under the wonderful upbuilding of the western sky. The light, the thick, heavy golden sunlight which is only seen in its full dripping splendour in town, spread on the desks and the floor like lacquer. I lifted my hands, to take the sunlight in them, smiling faintly to myself, trying to shut my fingers over its tangible richness.

Guidance to the above literary terms, answer keys to all the exercises and activities, plus a wealth of other reading-practice material, can be found at www.macmillanenglish.com/readers.

---

23 the mood that someone is in, which influences their attitudes or feelings

The Teddy-bears' Picnic

by William Trevor

About the author

William Trevor is an Irish writer of short stories, novels and plays. He was born on 24 May 1928 in Mitchelstown, County Cork, in the Republic of Ireland. His parents were middle-class Protestants, both bank clerks with farming ancestors[1], and they moved several times for work. Trevor attended 13 different schools during his childhood before finally finishing his education at St Columba's College in Dublin in 1946.

In 1950, Trevor graduated in history at Trinity College Dublin and then taught history at a school in Armagh, Northern Ireland for two years. He also started working as a sculptor under the name of Trevor Cox. In 1952, he married Jane Ryan and they moved to England two years later, where he worked first as an art teacher in Rugby and then Taunton, before moving to London in 1960 and finding work as a copywriter in an advertising agency.

Trevor's first novel, A Standard of Behaviour, was published in 1958, but did not do well. However, in 1964 his second novel, The Old Boys, won the prestigious Hawthornden Prize[2]. The commercial and critical success of this novel made it possible for Trevor to give up his copywriting job and dedicate himself to writing full-time. He and his family moved to a small village in Devon, in the south-west of England, where he has lived ever since.

Trevor's stories are set mainly in Ireland and England and include black comedies about eccentrics[3] and deviants, as well as stories exploring Irish history and politics – and especially the tensions between the Irish Protestant landowners and their Catholic tenants.

Trevor has written a number of highly successful novels, and several collections of short stories, many of which he has adapted as plays for the theatre, television and radio. His novels have won two Hawthornden

---

1 people related to you who lived a long time ago
2 a British literary award. It is one of the UK's oldest literary prizes and has been given annually since 1919
3 people who behave in slightly strange or unusual ways

Prizes and three Whitbread Awards[4], as well as being shortlisted for the Booker Prize[5] on four separate occasions. He was awarded a CBE[6] in 1977 and a knighthood[7] in 2002, both for his services to literature. In 2008, at the age of 80, he was awarded the Bob Hughes Lifetime Achievement Award in Irish Literature[8].

About the story

The Teddy-bears' Picnic was one of twelve stories published in the collection *Beyond the Pale and Other Stories* (Bodley Head, 1981).

Background information

The teddy-bears' picnic

Teddy bears, soft toys in the shape of a bear, are common children's toys all over the world. There are many examples of famous teddy bears in British children's literature, such as Pooh Bear (or Winnie the Pooh). The song *The teddy-bears' picnic* is a fantasy about a group of teddy bears having a picnic in the woods. It begins with a happy story of a group of teddy bears but ends with a dark warning – that although the picnic will be lovely, it would be better – and safer – to stay at home.

A desirable London suburb

The beginning of the story *The Teddy-bears' Picnic* is set in the London suburb of Wimbledon in south-west London. During the fortnight of the annual Wimbledon tennis championship the streets are crowded with visitors. There is a strong demand for homes in this area, especially in the Wimbledon Village and Wimbledon Park neighbourhoods, and house prices are among the highest in the outer London suburbs.

4 now known as the Costa Book Awards, a series of literary awards given to writers based in the UK and Ireland. They are awarded to works that help bring the enjoyment of reading to a wide audience
5 full name the Man Booker Prize for Fiction, a literary award given each year for the best English language novel written by a citizen of the Commonwealth, Ireland or Zimbabwe
6 Commander of the Order of the British Empire: a grade in the British order of merit, awarded by the Queen or government for services to the country
7 an honour awarded by the British state which allows a person to use the title *Sir* (male) or *Dame* (female) before their first name
8 an Irish literary award, originally sponsored by the Irish bookshop Hughes & Hughes

After World War II many of the large 19th century Victorian houses in Wimbledon Park were demolished and replaced with blocks of flats. In the story, a young, newly married couple, Edwin and Deborah, live in one of these blocks. It is important for them to have a distant view of Wimbledon Common, a large open space of beautiful parkland, from their flat. The view of the common makes their flat more valuable.

A picturesque English village

The story moves out of London to a village where Deborah grew up. The village is in South Buckinghamshire (South Bucks in the story), a wealthy rural area west of London. It is a beautiful area, with beech-tree woods on gentle chalk hills and small, well-tended villages full of old houses with beautiful gardens, like the one in the story.

The upper-middle class

The families in the story all belong to the upper-middle class. They have professional jobs (Edwin is a stockbroker – someone who works in the financial sector, buying and selling shares in companies for other people), they send their children to boarding school (private, residential schools) and they take pride in the symbols of their wealth and status. Edwin drives a Saab, but would like one day to own a Rover (at the time a British-made car which was considered a status symbol). Deborah buys their food at Marks and Spencer (a traditional British department store – the food from their food department is expensive but, at the time, it had a reputation for being fresh and fashionable). Edwin drinks whisky with a particular brand of soda water: Sparklets. And at dinner with Deborah's parents, they drink claret, an expensive French wine from the Bordeaux region of France. The family whose garden they use for the picnic are obviously very wealthy, as they have an extensive garden and a double-barrelled[9] surname, Ainley-Foxleton.

9 referring to two surnames joined by a hyphen. This is traditionally considered to be a mark of a wealthy family in Britain

Summary

It may help you to know something about what happens in the story before you read it. Don't worry, this summary does *not* tell you how the story ends!

Edwin and Deborah are a newly married couple. They live in a stylish flat in Wimbledon, West London. Edwin works as a stockbroker in the City (the financial area in the centre of London) and Deborah works as a secretary at a law firm.

One day a friend calls Deborah to invite her to a 'teddy-bears' picnic' with a group of friends from their childhood and their respective husbands and wives. The picnic is to take place in the village where Deborah grew up, at the home of an elderly couple who have a beautiful country garden.

Edwin is not happy about the invitation. He thinks the picnic is childish. He and Deborah argue about it, but in the end he agrees to go with her.

The picnic takes place as planned and the friends are enjoying themselves retelling stories from their shared pasts. However, Edwin is still not comfortable with the situation. He is still angry with his wife and her friends, and in his frustration he drinks too much – with tragic consequences.

Pre-reading activities

Key vocabulary

This section will help you familiarize yourself with some of the more specific vocabulary used in the story. You may want to use it to help you before you start reading, or as a revision exercise after you have finished the story.

Plants, flowers and gardens

The garden at the Ainley-Foxletons' home in the village plays an important role in the story, as do plants and flowers. Many plants and flowers are mentioned throughout the story, not only in the description of the garden.

1 Read the descriptions of the plants and flowers in the story. Which colours are mentioned most often? What overall image does this list give you of the garden in the story?

azalea a bush with pink, purple or yellow flowers, grown in gardens
broom a bush with small yellow flowers
buttercup a wild plant with small, bright, yellow flowers that often grows in grass
hollyhock a plant with tall stems and several large flowers on each stem
laburnum a tree with hanging yellow flowers that have poisonous seeds
petunia a garden plant with purple, pink or white flowers
rhododendron a large bush with big flowers and leaves that stay green all year
saponaria a plant which produces lots of small flowers which can be white, yellow, pink or pale purple
sea-pink a large pink flower that grows in clusters, mainly on rocky ground, and often on cliffs above the sea
thistle a wild plant with a thick, round purple or white flower and leaves with sharp points. It is often used as a symbol for Scotland
veronica a garden shrub which produces small, blue flowers

2 Read this description of the garden in the story. Match the words in bold with their definitions 1–6 below.

The garden itself is large and consists of various **lawns**, some **raised**, where the grass is tended very carefully. It also has a **rockery,** with plants that do not usually grow in grass, which is arranged in a semicircle with a **sundial** at its centre. At the bottom of the garden is a **shrubbery** and a small **glade,** which is where the picnic takes place.

1 an area, usually in a wood or forest, where there are no trees
2 areas of grass that are cut short, especially in someone's garden
3 higher than the area around it
4 a rock garden, where plants grow in and around rocks
5 an area in a garden where low thick bushes are planted
6 an object that measures time by the position of a shadow made in sunny weather

Key verbs

The story contains many verbs that describe specific movements, as well as moods.

3 Look at the list of verbs in the box below. Which of them:

1 have an object (are transitive)?
2 do not describe a movement involving arms or legs?
3 might suggest a bad mood?
4 might suggest a good mood?

---

amble off to walk away in a slow, relaxed way

giggle to laugh in a nervous, excited or silly way that is difficult to control

nudge to use your body, especially your elbow, to give a little push to someone or something

poke to push something quickly with your finger or a sharp object

poke forward to move a part of your body in the direction in front of you

potter (British) to do things in a slow and enjoyable way

slip away to leave secretly

stalk about to walk in a way that suggests you feel angry or offended

stroll about to walk around without hurrying, often for pleasure

sulk to show that you are angry about being treated badly by looking unhappy and not talking to anyone

tilt to move so that one side is higher than the other

wander off to move away from a place where people expect you to be

---

4 Use some of the verbs in exercise 3 to complete the extracts below. You may need to make some small changes to the spelling.

1 *It was something to .... over, not take so seriously.*
2 *Edwin ....d him with his elbow.*
3 *She considered it rude of Edwin to .... the room just because he'd had a bad day.*
4 *The heavily carpeted floor ....ed beneath him, falling away to the left and then to the right.*
5 *Nobody had noticed when he'd ....ed ....*
6 *'What are these?' he said, ...ing at a brown noodle with his fork.*

Idiomatic expressions

5 **Look at the extracts (a–g) from the story, then match the idiomatic phrases in bold with their definitions (1–7) below.**

a) *Mrs Chalm was known to be a woman who didn't go in for cant when dealing with the lives of the children she had borne and brought up; she* **made no bones about** *it and often said so.*

b) *Yet in the end Edwin and Deborah had married, one Tuesday afternoon in December, and Mrs Chalm resolved to* **make the best of** *it.*

c) *Edwin could not bear to lose and would* **go to ruthless lengths** *to ensure that he never did.*

d) *The chops … were fairly black, and* **serve him right** *for upsetting her.*

e) *Deborah* **thought the world of** *him, which was something she often said.*

f) *The quarrel had caused him to* **feel out of his depth**. *He should have been able to sort out such nonsense within a few minutes.*

g) *She was making the point that she had only to* **lift her little finger**, *that his cleverness was nothing compared with his love for her.*

1 to feel unable to deal with a situation because it is too difficult
2 to try in a very determined and unreasonable way to achieve something
3 to be able to make someone do something when you want them to
4 to talk about or do something in a very open way without feeling ashamed or embarrassed
5 (*British*): to accept a bad or difficult situation without complaining and try to deal with it as well as you can
6 used for saying that you think someone deserves something unpleasant that happens to them
7 to love someone very much

6 **Complete the sentences below with an idiomatic expression from exercise 5. Make any necessary changes to the words.**

1 I love her so much. She just has to .... and I'll do whatever she wants.
2 I've told you more than once not to climb that tree, so if you fall and hurt yourself, it'll ....
3 He .... his grandfather and really looked forward to his visits.
4 We are in a very difficult situation but there's nothing we can do to improve it. We'll just have to .... it.
5 Some athletes are prepared to .... to achieve success.
6 I had never been asked to speak in public before and I .... completely ....
7 She's always incredibly frank about everything and .... telling you if something's wrong.

Main themes

Before you read the story, you may want to think about some of its main themes. The questions will help you think about the story as you are reading it for the first time. There is more discussion of the main themes in the *Literary analysis* section after the story.

Married life

The two main characters, Edwin and Deborah, have only just married and have not yet settled into (become comfortable with) married life.

7 **As you read the story, ask yourself:**

a) Do you think they were right to get married? Do you think they will be happy together?
b) Do they manage their relationship well as newlyweds?

Appropriate behaviour

The story is set in an upper-middle-class setting, where behaviour and appropriacy[10] of behaviour is seen as being important.

8 As you read the story consider the following questions:

a) Why does Edwin think the teddy-bears' picnic is inappropriate? Do you agree with him?

b) In what way is Edwin's behaviour at the picnic inappropriate?

Childhood and growing up

The theme of growing up and the influence that our pasts have on us is a common one throughout literature, particularly in the 20th century. The story centres on a childhood tradition that has been carried on into adulthood, the teddy-bears' picnic, and it also contrasts two garden parties: one during the characters' childhood and another when they have grown up.

9 As you read the story, ask yourself:

a) What are the two main characters' attitudes to childhood and childhood traditions? What memories do they both have of their childhoods?

b) Which of the two main characters do you think is the most mature and grown-up?

10 the degree to which behaviour is natural or acceptable in a particular situation

The Teddy-bears' Picnic

by William Trevor

'I simply don't believe it,' Edwin said. 'Grown-up people?'

'Well, grown-up now, darling. We weren't always grown-up.'

'But teddy-bears, Deborah?'

'I'm sure I've told you dozens of times before.'

Edwin shook his head, **frowning** and staring at his wife. They'd been married six months: he was twenty-nine, swiftly making his way in a stockbroker's office, Deborah was twenty-six and intended to continue being Mr Harridance's secretary until a family began to come along. They lived in Wimbledon, in a block of flats called The Zodiac. 23 The Zodiac their address was and friends thought the title amusing and lively, making jokes about Gemini and Taurus and Capricorn when they came to drinks. A Dane had designed The Zodiac in 1968.

'I'll absolutely tell you this,' Edwin said, 'I'm not attending this thing.'

'But darling –'

'Oh, don't be bloody silly, Deborah.'

Edwin's mother had called Deborah 'a pretty little thing', implying for those who cared to be perceptive a certain **reservation**. She'd been more direct with Edwin himself, in a private conversation they'd had after Edwin had said he and Deborah wanted to get married. 'Remember, dear,' was how Mrs Chalm had put it then, 'she's not always going to be a pretty little thing. This really isn't a very sensible marriage, Edwin.' Mrs Chalm was known to be a woman who didn't go in for cant[11] when dealing with the lives of the children she had borne[12] and brought up; she made no bones about it and often said so. Her husband, on the other hand, kept out of things.

---

11 *rare:* talk that is not sincere, often about religion or morals
12 *formal:* given birth to

Yet in the end Edwin and Deborah had married, one Tuesday afternoon in December, and Mrs Chalm resolved to make the best of it. She advised Deborah about this and that, she gave her potted plants for 23 The Zodiac, and in fact was kind. If Deborah had known about her mother-in-law's doubts she'd have been surprised.

'But we've always done it, Edwin. All of us.'

'All of who, for heaven's sake?'

'Well, Angela for one. And Holly and Jeremy of course.'

'*Jeremy?* My God!'

'And Peter. And Enid and Pansy and Harriet.'

'You've never told me a word about this, Deborah.'

'I'm really sure I have.'

The sitting-room where this argument took place had a single huge window with a distant view of Wimbledon Common. The walls were covered with plum-coloured hessian[13], the floor with a plum-coloured carpet. The Chalms were still acquiring furniture: what there was, reflecting the style of The Zodiac's architecture, was in **bent** steel and glass. There was a single picture, of a field of thistles, revealed to be a photograph on closer examination. Bottles of alcohol stood on a glass-topped table, their colourful labels cheering that corner up. Had the Chalms lived in a Victorian flat, or a cottage in a mews[14], their sitting-room would have been different, **fussier** and more ornate, dictated by the architectural environment. Their choice of décor and furniture was the choice of newlyweds who hadn't yet discovered a confidence of their own.

'You mean you all sit round with your teddies,' Edwin said, 'having a picnic? And you'll still be doing that at eighty?'

'What d'you mean, eighty?'

'When you're eighty years of age, for God's sake. You're trying to tell me you'll still be going to this garden when you're **stumbling** about and hard of hearing, a gang of O.A.P.s[15]

13 *British*: a thick rough cloth used for making things such as bags and ropes, made from a plant, either hemp or jute
14 *British*: a small street with houses, especially one where there used to be stables for horses
15 old age pensioners: people who are old enough to receive a pension from the government

squatting out on the grass with teddy-bears?'

'I didn't say anything about when we're old.'

'You said it's a tradition, for God's sake.'

He poured some whisky into a glass and added a **squirt** of soda from a Sparklets **siphon**. Normally he would have poured a gin and dry vermouth for his wife, but this evening he felt too cross to bother. He hadn't had the easiest of days. There'd been an error in the office about the B.A.T.[16] shares a client had wished to buy, and he hadn't managed to have any lunch because as soon as the B.A.T. thing was sorted out a crisis had blown up over sugar **speculation**. It was almost eight o'clock when he'd got back to The Zodiac and instead of preparing a meal Deborah had been on the telephone to her friend Angela, talking about teddy-bears.

Edwin was an agile young man with shortish[17] black hair and a face that had a very slight look of an alligator about it. He was vigorous and athletic, **sound** on the tennis court, fond of squash and recently of golf. His mother had once stated that Edwin could not bear to lose and would go to ruthless lengths to ensure that he never did. She had even remarked to her husband that she hoped this quality would not one day cause trouble, but her husband replied it was probably just what a stockbroker needed. Mrs Chalm had been thinking more of personal relationships, where losing couldn't be avoided. It was that she'd had on her mind when she'd had doubts about the marriage, for the doubts were not there simply because Deborah was a pretty little thing: it was the conjunction Mrs Chalm was alarmed about.

'I didn't happen to get any lunch,' Edwin **snappishly** said now. 'I've had a long, unpleasant day and when I get back here –'

'I'm sorry, dear.'

Deborah immediately rose from among the plum-coloured cushions of the sofa and went to the kitchen, where she took two pork chops from a Marks and Spencer's carrier-bag and placed them under the grill of the electric cooker. She took a

16 British American Tobacco
17 quite short. The suffix *-ish* can be added to adjectives to make other adjectives meaning slightly or fairly

packet of frozen broccoli spears from the carrier-bag as well, and two Marks and Spencer's **trifles**. While typing letters that afternoon she'd planned to have fried noodles with the chops and broccoli spears, just for a change. A week ago they'd had fried noodles in the new Mexican place they'd found and Edwin said they were lovely. Deborah had kicked off her shoes as soon as she'd come into the flat and hadn't put them on since. She was wearing a dress with scarlet petunias on it. Dark-haired, with a heart-shaped face and blue eyes that occasionally acquired a **bewildered** look, she seemed several years younger than twenty-six, more like eighteen.

She put on water to boil for the broccoli spears even though the chops would not be ready for some time. She prepared a saucepan of oil for the noodles, hoping that this was the way to go about frying them. She couldn't understand why Edwin was making such a **fuss** just because Angela had telephoned, and **put it down to** his not having managed to get any lunch.

In the sitting-room Edwin stood by the huge window, surveying the tops of trees and, in the distance, Wimbledon Common. She must have been on the phone to Angela for an hour and a half, probably longer. He'd tried to ring himself to say he'd be late but each time the line had been engaged. He searched his mind carefully, going back through the three years he'd known Deborah, but no reference to a teddy-bears' picnic came to him. He'd said very positively that she had never mentioned it, but he'd said that in anger, just to make his point: reviewing their many conversations now, he saw he had been right and felt triumphant. Of course he'd have remembered such a thing, any man would.

Far down below, a car turned into the wide courtyard of The Zodiac, a Rover it looked like, a discreet shade of green. It wouldn't be all that long before they had a Rover themselves, even allowing for the fact that the children they hoped for would be arriving any time now. Edwin had not objected to Deborah continuing her work after their marriage, but family life would naturally be much tidier when she no longer could, when the children were born. Eventually they'd have to move into a house with a garden because it was natural that Deborah would want that, and he had no intention of disagreeing with her.

'Another thing is,' he said, moving from the window to the open doorway of the kitchen, 'how come you haven't had a reunion all the years I've known you? If it's an annual thing –'

'It isn't an annual thing, Edwin. We haven't had a picnic since 1975 and before that 1971. It's just when someone feels like it, I suppose. It's just a bit of fun, darling.'

'You call sitting down with teddy-bears a bit of fun? Grown-up people?'

'I wish you wouldn't keep on about grown-ups. I know we're grown-ups. That's the whole point. When we were little we all **vowed** –'

'Jesus Christ!'

He turned and went to pour himself another drink. She'd never mentioned it because she knew it was silly. She was ashamed of it, which was something she would discover when she grew up a bit.

'You know I've got Binky,' she said, following him to where the drinks were and pouring herself some gin. 'I've told you hundreds of times how I took him everywhere. If you don't like him in the bedroom I'll put him away. I didn't know you didn't like him.'

'I didn't say that, Deborah. It's completely different, what you're saying. It's private for a start. I mean, it's your teddy-bear and you've told me how fond you were of it. That's completely different from sitting down with a crowd of idiots –'

'They're not idiots, Edwin, actually.'

'Well, they certainly don't sound like anything else. D'you mean Jeremy and Peter are going to arrive **clutching** teddy-bears and then sit down on the grass pretending to feed them biscuit crumbs? For God's sake, Jeremy's a medical *doctor*!'

'Actually, nobody'll sit on the grass because the grass will probably be damp. Everyone brought rugs last time. It's really because of the garden, you know. It's probably the nicest garden in South Bucks, and then there're the Ainley-Foxletons. I mean, they do so love it all.'

He'd actually been in the garden, and he'd once actually met the Ainley-Foxletons. One Saturday afternoon during his **engagement** to Deborah there had been tea on a raised lawn. Laburnum and broom were out, a mass of yellow everywhere. Quite pleasant old sticks[18] the Ainley-Foxletons had been, but neither of them had mentioned a teddy-bears' picnic.

'I think she did as a matter of fact,' Deborah mildly insisted. 'I remember because I said it hadn't really been so long since the last one – eighteen months ago would it be when I took you to see them? Well, 1975 wasn't all that long before that, and she said it seemed like aeons[19]. I remember her saying that, I remember "aeons" and thinking it just like her to come out with a word people don't use any more.'

'And you never thought to point out the famous picnic site? For hours we walked round and round that garden and yet it never occurred to you –'

'We didn't walk round and round. I'm sorry you were bored, Edwin.'

'I didn't say I was bored.'

'I know the Ainley-Foxletons can't hear properly and it's a **strain**, but you said you wanted to meet them –'

'I didn't say anything of the kind! You kept telling me about these people and their house and garden, but I can assure you I wasn't **crying out to** meet them in any way whatsoever. In fact, I rather wanted to play tennis that afternoon.'

'You didn't say so at the time.'

'Of course I didn't say so.'

'Well, then.'

'What I'm trying to get through to you is that we walked round and round that garden even though it had begun to rain. And not once did you say, "That's where we used to have our famous teddy-bears' picnic."'

18 *British, informal, old-fashioned:* people
19 *rare:* a very long time

'As a matter of fact I think I did. And it isn't famous. I wish you wouldn't keep on about it being famous.'

Deborah poured herself more gin and added the same amount of dry vermouth to the glass. She considered it rude of Edwin to stalk about the room just because he'd had a bad day, drinking himself and not bothering about her. If he hadn't liked the poor old Ainley-Foxletons he should have said so. If he'd wanted to play tennis that afternoon he should have said so too.

'Well, be all that as it may,' he was saying now, rather **pompously** in Deborah's opinion, 'I do not intend to take part in any of this nonsense.'

'But everybody's husband will, and the wives too. It's only fun, darling.'

'Oh, do stop saying it's fun. You sound like a **half-wit**. And something's smelling in the kitchen.'

'I don't think that's very nice, Edwin. I don't see why you should call me a half-wit.'

'Listen, I've had an extremely unpleasant day –'

'Oh, do stop about your stupid old day.'

She carried her glass to the kitchen with her and removed the chops from beneath the grill. They were fairly black, and serve him right for upsetting her. Why on earth did he have to make such a fuss, why couldn't he be like everyone else? It was something to giggle over, not take so seriously, a single Sunday afternoon when they wouldn't be doing anything anyway. She dropped a handful of noodles into the hot oil and then a second handful.

In the sitting-room the telephone rang just as Edwin was squirting soda into another drink. 'Yes?' he said, and Angela's voice came **lilting** over the line, saying she didn't want to bother Debbie but the date had just been fixed: June 17th. 'Honestly, you'll **split your sides**, Edwin.'

'Yes, all right, I'll tell her,' he said as coldly as he could. He replaced the receiver without saying goodbye. He'd never cared for Angela, **patronizing** kind of creature.

Deborah knew it had been Angela on the telephone and she knew she would have given Edwin the date she had arranged with Pansy and Peter, who'd been the doubtful ones about the first date, suggested by Jeremy. Angela had said she was going to ring back with this information, but when the Chalms sat down to their chops and broccoli spears and noodles Edwin hadn't yet passed the information on.

'Christ, what are these?' he said, poking at a brown noodle with his fork and then poking at the burnt chop.

'The little things are fried noodles, which you enjoyed so much the other night. The larger thing is a pork chop, which wouldn't have got overcooked if you hadn't started an argument.'

'Oh, for God's sake!'

He pushed his chair back and stood up. He returned to the sitting-room and Deborah heard the squirting of the soda siphon. She stood up herself, followed him to the sitting-room and poured herself another gin and vermouth. Neither of them spoke. Deborah returned to the kitchen and ate her share of the broccoli spears. The sound of the television came from the sitting-room. 'Listen, buster[20], you give this bread[21] to the hit[22] or don't you?' a voice demanded. 'OK, I give the bread,' a second voice replied.

They'd had quarrels before. They'd quarrelled on their honeymoon in Greece for no reason whatsoever. They'd quarrelled because she'd once left the ignition of the car turned on, causing a flat battery. They'd quarrelled because of Enid's boring party just before Christmas. The present quarrel was just the same kind of thing, Deborah knew: Edwin would sit and sulk, she'd wash the dishes up feeling miserable, and he'd probably eat the chop and the broccoli when they were cold. She couldn't blame him for not wanting the noodles because she didn't seem to have cooked them correctly. Then she thought: what if he doesn't come to the picnic, what if he just goes on being stubborn, which he could be when he wanted to? Everyone would know. 'Where's Edwin?' they would ask,

20 *very informal, mainly US*: an impolite word used when talking to a man whose name you do not know
21 *informal, old-fashioned*: money
22 *very informal, mainly US*: someone who kills for someone else, usually for money

and she'd tell some lie and everyone would know it was a lie, everyone would know they weren't getting on. Only six months had passed, everyone would say, and he wouldn't join in a bit of fun.

But to Deborah's relief that didn't happen. Later that night Edwin ate the cold pork chop, eating it from his fingers because he couldn't manage to stick a fork into it. He ate the cold broccoli spears as well, but he left the noodles. She made him tea and gave him a Danish pastry and in the morning he said he was sorry.

———

'So if we could it would be lovely,' Deborah said on her office telephone. She'd told her mother there was to be another teddy-bears' picnic, Angela and Jeremy had arranged it mainly, and the Ainley-Foxletons would love it of course, possibly the last they'd see.

'My dear, you're always welcome, as you know.' The voice of Deborah's mother came all the way from South Bucks, from the village where the Ainley-Foxletons' house and garden were, where Deborah and Angela, Jeremy, Pansy, Harriet, Enid, Peter and Holly had been children together. The plan was that Edwin and Deborah should spend the weekend of June 17th with Deborah's parents, and Deborah's mother had even promised to lay on some tennis for Edwin on the Saturday. Deborah herself wasn't much good at tennis.

'Thanks, Mummy,' she managed to say just as Mr Harridance returned from lunch.

'No, spending the whole weekend actually,' Edwin informed his mother. 'There's this teddy-bear thing Deborah has to go to.'

'What teddy-bear thing?'

Edwin went into details explaining how the children who'd been friends in a South Bucks village nearly twenty years ago met from time to time to have a teddy-bears' picnic because that was what they'd done then.

'But they're adults surely now,' Mrs Chalm pointed out.

'Yes, I know.'

'Well, I hope you have a lovely time, dear.'

'Delightful, I'm sure.'

'It's **odd** when they're adults, I'd have thought.'

Between themselves, Edwin and Deborah did not again discuss the subject of the teddy-bears' picnic. During the quarrel Edwin had felt bewildered, never quite knowing how to proceed, and he hoped that on some future occasion he would be better able to cope. It made him angry when he wasn't able to cope, and the anger still hung about him. On the other hand, six months wasn't long in a marriage which he hoped would go on for ever: the marriage hadn't had a chance to settle into the shape that suited it, any more than he and Deborah had had time to develop their own taste in furniture and decoration. It was only to be expected that there should be problems and uncertainty.

As for Deborah, she knew nothing about marriages settling into shape: she wasn't aware that rules and **tacit** understandings, arrangements of give and take, were what made marriage possible when the first gloss had worn off. Marriage for Deborah was the continuation of a love affair, and as yet she had few complaints. She knew that of course they had to have quarrels.

They had met at a party. Edwin had left a group of people he was listening to and had crossed to the corner where she was being bored by a man in computers. 'Hullo,' Edwin just said. All three of them were eating plates of paella.

Finding a consideration of the past pleasanter than speculation about the future, Deborah often recalled that moment: Edwin's eager face smiling at her, the computer man discomfited[23], a sour taste in the paella. 'You're not Fiona's sister?' Edwin said, and when ages afterwards she'd asked him who Fiona was he confessed he'd made her up. 'I shouldn't eat much more of this stuff,' he said, taking the paella away from her. Deborah had been impressed by that: she and the computer man had been **fiddling at** the paella with their forks, both of them too polite to say that there was something the matter with it. 'What do you

23 *literary:* made to feel embarrassed

do?' Edwin said a few minutes later, which was more than the computer man had asked.

In the weeks that followed they told one another all about themselves, about their parents and the houses they'd lived in as children, the schools they'd gone to, the friends they'd made. Edwin was a darling person, he was successful, he liked to be in charge of things. Without in any way sounding boastful, he told her of episodes in his childhood, of risks taken at school. Once he'd **dismantled** the elderly music master's bed, causing it to collapse when the music master later lay down on it. He'd removed the **carburettor** from some other master's car, he'd stolen an egg-beater from an ironmonger's shop. All of them were dares[24], and by the end of his schooldays he had acquired the reputation of being fearless; there was nothing, people said, he wouldn't do.

It was easy for Deborah to love him, and everything he told her, **self-deprecatingly couched**, was clearly the truth. But Deborah in love naturally didn't wonder how this side of Edwin would seem in marriage, nor how it might develop as Edwin moved into middle age. She couldn't think of anything nicer than having him there every day, and in no way did she feel **let down** on their honeymoon in Greece or by the couple of false starts they made with flats before they eventually ended up in 23 The Zodiac. Edwin went to his office every day and Deborah went to hers. That he told her more about share prices than she told him about the letters she typed for Mr Harridance was because share prices were more important. It was true that she would often have quite liked to pass on details of this or that, for instance of the correspondence with Flitts, Hay and Co. concerning nearly eighteen thousand defective chair **castors**. The correspondence was interesting because it had continued for two years and had become vituperative[25]. But when she mentioned it Edwin just agreeably nodded. There was also the business about Miss Royal's **scratches**, which everyone in the

24 a childhood game, where a child has to do something dangerous or scary to show that they are brave
25 *very formal*: full of cruel angry criticisms and insults

office had been conjecturing[26] about: how on earth had a woman like Miss Royal acquired four long scratches on her face and neck between five-thirty one Monday evening and nine-thirty the following morning? 'Oh yes?' Edwin had said, and gone on to talk about the Mercantile Investment Trust.

Deborah did not recognize these **telltale** signs. She did not remember that when first she and Edwin exchanged information about one another's childhoods Edwin had sometimes just smiled, as if his mind had **drifted** away. It was only a slight disappointment that he didn't wish to hear about Flitts, Hay and Co., and Miss Royal's scratches; no one could possibly **get into a state** about things like that. Deborah saw little significance in the silly quarrel they'd had about the teddy-bears' picnic, which was silly itself of course. She didn't see that it had had to do with friends who were hers and not Edwin's; nor did it occur to her that when they really began to think about the decoration of 23 The Zodiac it would be Edwin who would make the decisions. They shared things, Deborah would have said: after all, in spite of the quarrel they were going to go to the teddy-bears' picnic, Edwin loved her and was kind and really rather marvellous. It was purely for her sake that he'd agreed to give up a whole weekend.

So on a warm Friday afternoon, as they drove from London in their Saab, Deborah was feeling happy. She listened while Edwin talked about a killing[27] a man called Dupree had made by selling out his International Asphalt holding. 'James James Morrison Morrison Weatherby George Dupree[28],' she said.

'What on earth's that?'

'It's by A.A. Milne[29], the man who wrote about Pooh Bear. Poor Pooh!'

Edwin didn't say anything.

'Jeremy's is called Pooh.'

'I see.'

26 *formal*: deciding if something is true or likely based on the information that you have

27 *very informal*: a lot of money

28 a line from a poem called *Disobedience* by A. A. Milne (see note 29)

29 an English author best known for his books about the teddy-bear Winnie the Pooh

In the back of the car, propped up in a corner, was the blue teddy-bear called Binky which Deborah had had since she was one.

———

The rhododendrons were **in bloom** in the Ainley-Foxletons' garden, late that year because of the bad winter. So was the laburnum Edwin remembered, and the broom, and some yellow azaleas. 'My dear, we're so awfully glad,' old Mrs Ainley-Foxleton said, kissing him because she imagined he must be one of the children in her past. Her husband, **tottering** about on the raised lawn which Edwin also remembered from his previous visit, had developed **the shakes**. 'Darlings, Mrs Bright has ironed our tablecloth for us,' Mrs Ainley-Foxleton announced with a **flourish**.

She imparted this fact because Mrs Bright, the Ainley-Foxletons' char-woman[30], was emerging at that moment from the house, with the ironed tablecloth over one arm. She carried a tray on which there were glass jugs of orange **squash** and lemon squash, a jug of milk, mugs with Beatrix Potter[31] characters on them, and two plates of sandwiches that weren't much larger than postage stamps. She made her way down stone steps from the raised lawn, crossed a more extensive lawn and disappeared into a shrubbery. While everyone remained chattering to the Ainley-Foxletons – nobody helping to lay the picnic out because that had never been part of the **proceedings** – Mrs Bright reappeared from the shrubbery, returned to the house and then made a second journey, her tray laden[32] this time with cake and biscuits.

Before lunch Edwin had sat for a long time with Deborah's father in the summer-house, drinking. This was something Deborah's father enjoyed on Sunday mornings, permitting himself a degree of **dozy** inebriation[33] which only became

30 *British, old-fashioned:* cleaner
31 an English author and illustrator best known for her children's books about animals like Peter Rabbit
32 *mainly literary:* carrying something heavy, or supporting the weight of something heavy
33 *formal:* drunkenness

noticeable when two bottles of claret were consumed at lunch. Today Edwin had followed his example, twice getting to his feet to refill their glasses and during the course of lunch managing to slip out to the summer-house for a fairly heavy tot[34] of whisky, which mixed nicely with the claret. He could think of no other condition in which to present himself – with a teddy-bear Deborah's mother had pressed upon him – in the Ainley-Foxletons' garden. 'Rather you than me, old chap,' Deborah's father had said after lunch, subsiding[35] into an armchair with a **gurgle**. At the last moment Edwin had quickly returned to the summer-house and had helped himself to a further intake of whisky, drinking from the cap of the Teacher's[36] bottle because the glasses had been collected up. He reckoned that when Mrs Ainley-Foxleton had kissed him he must have smelt like a distillery, and he was glad of that.

'Well, here we are,' Jeremy said in the glade where the picnic had first taken place in 1957. He sat at the head of the tablecloth, cross-legged on a **tartan** rug. He had glasses and was **stout**. Peter at the other end of the tablecloth didn't seem to have grown much in the intervening years, but Angela had **shot up** like a hollyhock and in fact resembled one. Enid was **dumpy**, Pansy almost beautiful; Harriet had **protruding** teeth, Holly was **bouncy**. Jeremy's wife and Peter's wife, and Pansy's husband – a man in Shell[37] – all entered into the spirit of the occasion. So did Angela's husband, who came from Czechoslovakia and must have found the proceedings peculiar, everyone sitting there with a teddy-bear that had a name. Angela put a record on Mrs Ainley-Foxleton's old wind-up gramophone[38]. 'Oh, don't go down to the woods today,' a voice **screeched**, 'without consulting me.'[39] Mr and Mrs Ainley-Foxleton were due to arrive at the scene later, as was the tradition. They came with chocolates apparently, and

34 a glass, or measure, of whisky
35 *poetic use:* sinking
36 a brand of whisky
37 an oil company
38 *old-fashioned:* a machine for playing vinyl records
39 a combination of the words form the original song, *The teddy-bears' picnic*, and the A. A. Milne poem, *Disobedience* (see note 28)

bunches of buttercups for the teddy-bears.

'Thank you, Edwin,' Deborah whispered while the music and the song continued. She wanted him to remember the quarrel they'd had about the picnic; she wanted him to know that she now truly forgave him, and appreciated that in the end he'd seen the fun of it all.

'Listen, I have to go to the lav[40],' Edwin said. 'Excuse me for a minute.' Nobody except Deborah seemed to notice when he ambled off because everyone was talking so, exchanging news.

———

The anger which had hung about Edwin after the quarrel had never evaporated. It was in anger that he had telephoned his mother, and further anger had smacked at him when she'd said she hoped he would have a lovely time. What she had meant was that she'd told him so: marry a pretty little thing and **before you can blink** you're sitting down to tea with teddy-bears. You're a fool to put up with rubbish like this was what Deborah's father had meant when he'd said rather you than me.

Edwin did not lack brains and he had always been aware of it. It was his cleverness that was still offended by what he considered to be an embarrassment, a kind of **gooey** awfulness in an elderly couple's garden. At school he had always hated anything to do with **dressing up,** he'd even felt awkward when he'd had to read poetry aloud. What Edwin admired was solidity: he liked Westminster and the City, he liked trains moving smoothly, suits and clean shirts. When he'd married Deborah he'd known – without having to be told by his mother – that she was not a clever person, but in Edwin's view a clever wife was far from necessary. He had seen a future in which children were born and educated, in which Deborah developed various cooking and housekeeping skills, in which together they gave small dinner-parties. Yet instead of that, after only six months, there was this **grotesque** absurdity. Getting drunk wasn't a regular occurrence with Edwin: he drank when he was angry, as he had on the night of the quarrel.

40 *British, informal:* shortened version of lavatory, toilet

Mr Ainley-Foxleton was pottering about with his stick on the raised lawn, but Edwin took no notice of him. The old man appeared to be looking for something, his head poked forward on his **scrawny** neck, bespectacled[41] eyes examining the grass. Edwin passed into the house. From behind a closed door he could hear the voices of Mrs Ainley-Foxleton and Mrs Bright, talking about buttercups. He opened another door and entered the Ainley-Foxletons' dining-room. On the sideboard there was a row of **decanters**.

Edwin discovered that it wasn't easy to drink from a decanter, but he managed it none the less. Anger spurted in him all over again. It seemed incredible that he had married a girl who hadn't properly grown up. None of them had grown up, none of them desired to belong in the adult world, not even the husbands and wives who hadn't been involved in the first place. If Deborah had told him about any of it on that Sunday afternoon when they'd visited this house he wondered, even, if he would have married her.

Yet replacing the stopper of the decanter between mouthfuls in case anyone came in, Edwin found it impossible to admit that he had made a mistake in marrying Deborah: he loved her, he had never loved anyone else, and he doubted if he would ever love anyone else in the future. Often in an idle moment, between selling and buying in the office, he thought of her, seeing her in her different clothes and sometimes without any clothes at all. When he returned to 23 The Zodiac he sometimes put his arms around her and would not let her go until he had laid her gently down on their bed. Deborah thought the world of him, which was something she often said.

In spite of all that it was extremely annoying that the quarrel had caused him to feel out of his depth. He should have been able to sort out such nonsense within a few minutes; he deserved his mother's **gibe** and his father-in-law's as well. Even though they'd only been married six months, it was absurd that since Deborah loved him so he hadn't been able to make her see how

41 *formal:* wearing glasses

foolish she was being. It was absurd to be standing here drunk.

The Ainley-Foxletons' dining-room, full of silver and polished furniture and dim oil paintings, shifted out of focus. The row of decanters became two rows and then one again. The heavily carpeted floor tilted beneath him, falling away to the left and then to the right. Deborah had let him down. She had brought him here so that he could be displayed in front of Angela and Jeremy and Pansy, Harriet, Holly, Enid, Peter, and the husbands and the wives. She was making the point that she had only to lift her little finger, that his cleverness was nothing compared with his love for her. The anger hammered at him now, hurting him almost. He wanted to walk away, to drive the Saab back to London and when Deborah followed him to state quite categorically that if she intended to be a fool there would have to be a divorce. But some part of Edwin's anger insisted that such a course of action would be an admission of failure and defeat. It was absurd that the marriage he had chosen to make should end before it had properly begun, due to silliness.

Edwin took a last mouthful of whisky and replaced the glass stopper. He remembered another social occasion, years ago, and he was struck by certain similarities with the present one. People had given a garden party in aid of some charity or other which his mother liked to support, to which he and his brother and sister, and his father, had been **dragged along**. It had been an **excruciatingly** boring afternoon, in the middle of a heatwave. He'd had to wear his **floppy** cotton hat, which he hated, and an awful tan-coloured summer suit, made of cotton also. There had been hours and hours of just standing while his mother talked to people, sometimes slowly giving them recipes, which they wrote down. Edwin's brother and sister didn't seem to mind that; his father did as he was told. So Edwin had wandered off, into a house that was larger and more handsome than the Ainley-Foxletons'. He'd strolled about in the downstairs rooms, eaten some jam he found in the kitchen, and then gone upstairs to the bedrooms. He'd **rooted around** for a while, opening drawers and wardrobes, and then he'd climbed a flight of uncarpeted stairs to a **loft**. From there he'd made his way out on to the roof. Edwin had almost forgotten this incident and certainly never **dwelt on** it, but with a vividness that surprised him it now returned.

He left the dining-room. In the hall he could still hear the voices of Mrs Ainley-Foxleton and Mrs Bright. Nobody had bothered with him that day; his mother, whose favourite he had always been, was even impatient when he said he had a toothache. Nobody had noticed when he'd slipped away. But from the **parapet** of the roof everything had been different. The faces of the people were pale, similar dots, all gazing up at him. The colours of the women's dresses were confused among the flowers. Arms waved frantically at him; someone shouted, ordering him to come down.

On the raised lawn the old man was still examining the grass, his head still poked down towards it, his stick **prodding** at it. From the glade where the picnic was taking place came a brief burst of applause, as if someone had just made a speech. '…today's the day the teddy-bears have their picnic,' sang the screeching voice, faintly.

A breeze had cooled Edwin's sunburnt arms as he crept along the parapet. He'd sensed his mother's first realization that it was he, and noticed his brother's and sister's weeping. He had seen his father summoned from the car where he'd been dozing. Edwin had stretched his arms out, balancing like a **tightrope** performer. All the boredom, the **tiresome** heat, the cotton hat and suit, were easily made up for. Within minutes it had become his day.

'Well, it's certainly the weather for it,' Edwin said to the old man.

'Eh?'

'The weather's nice,' he shouted. 'It's a fine day.'

'There's fungus[42] in this lawn, you know. Eaten up with it.' Mr Ainley-Foxleton investigated small black patches with his stick. 'Never knew there was fungus here,' he said.

---

42 *biological*: a type of plant without leaves, flowers or green colour that grows mainly in wet places or on decaying substances. There are many types of fungi, including mushrooms, mildews, yeasts and moulds

They were close to the edge of the lawn. Below them there was a rockery full of veronica and sea-pinks and saponaria. The rockery was arranged in a semicircle, around a sundial.

'Looks like fungus there too,' Edwin said, pointing at the larger lawn that stretched away beyond this rockery.

'Eh?' The old man **peered** over the edge, not knowing what he was looking for because he hadn't properly heard. 'Eh?' he said again, and Edwin nudged him with his elbow. The stick went flying off at an angle, the old man's head struck the edge of the sundial with a sharp, clean crack. 'Oh, don't go down to the woods today,' the voice began again, drifting through the sunshine over the scented garden. Edwin glanced quickly over the windows of the house in case there should be a face at one of them. Not that it would matter: at that distance no one could see such a slight movement of the elbow.

––––––

They ate banana sandwiches and egg sandwiches, and biscuits with icing on them, chocolate cake and coffee cake. The teddy-bears' **snouts** were pressed over the Beatrix Potter mugs, each teddy-bear addressed by name. Edwin's was called Tomkin.

'Remember the day of the thunderstorm?' Enid said, **screwing up her features** in a way she had – like a **twitch** really, Edwin considered. The day he had walked along the parapet might even have been the day of the thunderstorm, and he smiled because somehow that was amusing. Angela was smiling too, and so were Jeremy and Enid, Pansy, Harriet and Holly, Peter and the husbands and wives. Deborah in particular was smiling. When Edwin glanced from face to face he was reminded of the faces that had gazed up at him from so far below, except that there'd been panic instead of smiles.

'Remember the syrup?' Angela said. 'Poor Algernon had to be given a horrid bath.'

'Wasn't it Horatio, surely?' Deborah said.

'Yes, it was Horatio,' Enid confirmed, amusingly balancing Horatio on her shoulder.

'Today's the day the teddy-bears have their picnic,' suddenly sang everyone, taking a lead from the voice on the gramophone. Edwin smiled and even began to sing himself. When they returned to Deborah's parents' house the atmosphere would be sombre. 'Poor old **chap** was **overlooked**,' he'd probably be the one to explain, 'due to all that fuss.' And in 23 The Zodiac the atmosphere would be sombre also. 'I'm afraid you should get rid of it,' he'd suggest, arguing that the blue teddy-bear would be for ever a reminder. Grown up a bit because of what had happened, Deborah would of course agree. Like everything else, marriage had to settle into shape.

Pansy told a story of an adventure her Mikey had had when she'd taken him back to boarding-school, how a **repulsive** girl called Leonora Thorpe had stuck a **skewer** in him. Holly told of how she'd had to rescue her Percival from drowning when he'd **toppled** out of a motor-boat. Jeremy **wound up** the gramophone and the chatter **jollily** continued, the husbands and wives appearing to be as delighted as anyone. Harriet said how she'd only wanted to marry Peter and Peter how he was determined to marry Deborah. 'Oh, don't go down to the woods today,' the voice began again, and then came Mrs Ainley-Foxleton's scream.

Everyone rushed, leaving the teddy-bears just anywhere and the gramophone still playing. Edwin was the first to bend over the **splayed** figure of the old man. He declared that Mr Ainley-Foxleton was dead, and then took charge of the proceedings.

Post-reading activities

Understanding the story

Use these questions to help you check that you have understood the story.

Edwin and Deborah

1 What are Deborah and Edwin discussing at the beginning of the story?
2 How long have Deborah and Edwin been married?
3 What else do you learn about them in the opening paragraph?
4 What does Edwin's mother think of Deborah? And of their marriage?
5 What does his father think?
6 Does Deborah have a good relationship with her mother-in-law?
7 How does the decoration in the living room reflect the couple's relationship?
8 What aspect of Edwin's personality worries his mother? Why?
9 Who prepares the dinner? Why?
10 What are they having for dinner? What does this tell you about the cook?
11 What aspect of Deborah's appearance strikes you as being most interesting?
12 How does she explain Edwin's irritation to herself?
13 What is Edwin thinking about as he looks out of the living room window?
14 Why is Edwin so angered by the idea of the teddy-bears' picnic?
15 Who thinks the teddy-bears' picnic is silly: Edwin, Deborah, or both?
16 Who are the Ainley-Foxletons?
17 Where and when did the last picnic take place?
18 In what way is Edwin rude to Deborah? What words does she find particularly rude?
19 What has happened to the dinner while they have been arguing?
20 Who is Angela? What does she want? What is Edwin's attitude towards her?
21 What does Edwin do instead of eating his dinner? Why?
22 Is Deborah worried about their quarrel? Why/Why not?
23 How does the quarrel end?
24 In what way are Edwin and Deborah's feelings about the quarrel different?

25 How did Edwin and Deborah first meet?
26 What impressed Deborah about Edwin?
27 What stories did they tell each other?
28 What kind of things did Edwin do as a child? Was Deborah interested in his stories?
29 Is Edwin interested in Deborah's stories about work?
30 How does Deborah feel about her job compared to Edwin's? Why?
31 Was Edwin interested in Deborah's stories about her childhood?
32 Who is Dupree? Why is Edwin talking about him?
33 What does the name Dupree make Deborah think of?
34 What is Edwin's reaction to the change in the conversation?

The teddy-bears' picnic

35 How old do you think Mr and Mrs Ainley-Foxleton are? What do they do that is typical of people their age?
36 Who is preparing the picnic? Why don't the others help?
37 Where had Edwin and Deborah been before the picnic? What had Edwin been doing?
38 How many people are at the picnic? Are they all enjoying it?
39 Why aren't the Ainley-Foxletons there too?
40 Why does Edwin leave the picnic? Where does he go? Why?
41 What exactly is he angry about? What effect does the alcohol have on his mood?
42 Why does he suddenly remember a day from this past? What are the similarities between the teddy-bears' picnic and that day from his childhood?
43 What had he done that day to get everybody's attention?
44 Why does Edwin stop to talk to Mr Ainley-Foxleton? Is he polite to him?
45 What happens after Edwin nudges Mr Ainley-Foxleton?
46 What is everybody doing back at the picnic? What is the general mood?
47 What kind of mood is Edwin in? What is he thinking about?
48 What brings the picnic to an end?
49 Who takes charge of the proceedings?

Language study

The Teddy-bears' Picnic is a story about a developing relationship and a key event in its development. The young couple quarrel about the upcoming picnic mainly because they have very different views about what is, or isn't, appropriate behaviour, and about what people should or should not do. The story encourages us to ask similar questions about the couple's past decisions and actions.

Should have – criticizing past events

Form

should/shouldn't + *have* + past participle

Use

We use *should/shouldn't have* to talk about what you think would have been the best, the correct or the most appropriate thing to do in a past situation. The action described using *should have* is the opposite of what really happened:

If he hadn't liked the poor old Ainley-Foxletons, he should have said so.
(but he didn't say anything)
If he'd wanted to play tennis that afternoon, he should have said so too.
(but he didn't mention it until 18 months later during their quarrel about the picnic)
Should have is often used in the main clause of a conditional sentence, as above. However it can also be used on its own:
Edwin's mother should have persuaded him not to marry Deborah.

1 **Complete the sentences below using *should/shouldn't have* and the correct form of the verb in brackets.**

1 Maybe Edwin .... (marry) Deborah.
2 Edwin's mother .... (speak) to Deborah about her doubts.
3 Deborah .... (go) to the picnic on her own.
4 Edwin .... (refuse) to go to the party.
5 Deborah's father .... (offer) him so much wine at lunch.
6 Deborah .... (let) Edwin go off on his own.
7 Edwin definitely .... (have) so much to drink.
8 Maybe he .... (talk) to Deborah about his feelings.

2 Look again at the sentences in exercise 1. Do you agree with them? Why/Why not?

Past perfect – referring to previous events and actions

At various points throughout the story, both of the main characters think back to moments in the past, moments from their childhood or from early stages in their relationship. The past perfect is often used to signal a shift into the past.

Form

had/hadn't + past participle

Use

We use the past perfect to show that an action happened, or a situation existed, before a certain point in the past.

3 Look at the example of the past perfect below. What does the word *before* refer to?

> *They'd had quarrels before. They'd quarrelled on their honeymoon in Greece for no reason whatsoever.*

4 Complete the extract below using the past perfect form of the verbs in brackets.

*He .... (not/have) the easiest of days. There ....
(be) an error in the office about the B.A.T. shares a client ....
(wish) to buy, and he .... (not/manage) to have any lunch
because as soon as the B.A.T. thing was sorted out a crisis ....
(blow) up over sugar speculation. It was almost eight o'clock when he
.... (get) back to The Zodiac and instead of preparing a meal
Deborah .... (be) on the telephone to her friend Angela, talking
about teddy-bears.*

Compare your answers with the extract on page 44. Did you use contracted forms in the same places?

Formal vocabulary

The fact that the story is set in an upper-middle-class setting is reflected in the use of formal vocabulary. This is typical of a more formal style of middle-class speech.

5 Look at the words in bold in the extracts below. Match them with their more neutral equivalents in the box.

> combination   coming out   drunk   explained   looking at
> make sure   said   told   wanted   worried

1 *His mother had once **stated** that Edwin could not bear to lose and would go to ruthless lengths to **ensure** that he never did.*
2 *The doubts were not there simply because Deborah was a pretty little thing: it was the **conjunction** Mrs Chalm was **alarmed** about.*
3 *In the sitting-room Edwin stood by the huge window, **surveying** the tops of trees and, in the distance, Wimbledon Common.*
4 *'No, spending the whole weekend actually,' Edwin **informed** his mother. 'There's this teddy-bear thing Deborah has to go to.'*
5 *'Darlings, Mrs Bright has ironed our tablecloth for us,' Mrs Ainley-Foxleton announced with a flourish. She **imparted** this fact because Mrs Bright, the Ainley-Foxletons' char-woman, was **emerging** at that moment from the house.*
6 *Two bottles of claret were **consumed** at lunch.*
7 *None of them had grown up, none of them **desired** to belong in the adult world.*

6 Look again at the words in bold in exercise 5. How many are verbs? Which describe:

a) how someone is speaking?
b) what someone is doing?

What effect does this more formal vocabulary have on the descriptions of these people?

Upper-middle-class speech

7 Look at the extracts below. The words and phrases in brackets are typical of upper-middle-class, or refined, speech. Put them in the correct position in the extracts.

1 'I don't believe it,' Edwin said. 'Grown-up people?' (simply)
  'Well, grown-up now. We weren't always grown-up.' (darling) [Page 42]

2 'But we've always done it, Edwin. All of us.'
  'All of who?' (for heaven's sake) [Page 43]

3 'It's probably the nicest garden in South Bucks, and then there're the Ainley-Foxletons. I mean, they love it all.' (do so) [Page 47]

4 'You're always welcome, as you know.' The voice of Deborah's mother came all the way from South Bucks. (my dear) [Page 50]

5 'James James Morrison Morrison Weatherby George Dupree,' she said. 'What's that?' (on earth) [Page 53]

6 'Remember the syrup?' Angela said. 'Poor Algernon had to be given a bath.' (horrid) [Page 60]

Check your answers in the story.

Literary analysis

Plot

1 Look at the list of events in the story. Number them in the order they actually happened.

    a) Mr Ainley-Foxleton died.

    b) Edwin met Deborah.

    c) The first teddy-bears' picnic was held.

    d) Edwin climbed onto a rooftop at a garden party.

    e) Deborah first mentioned the teddy-bears' picnic to Edwin.

    f) Angela called Deborah to make arrangements for a teddy-bears' picnic.

    g) Edwin and Deborah got married.

    h) Edwin first visited the Ainley-Foxletons.

    i) Edwin and Deborah had lunch at Deborah's parents' home.

    j) Edwin and Deborah argued about the picnic.

2 Look again at the list of events in exercise 1. What event is missing? Which do you think are the three most important events? Why? In what way could the other events be seen as important to the story?

3 How many different past events (i.e. those that happened before the time of the story) are described? How does each of these past events help us to understand the relationship between Edwin and Deborah and what eventually happened at the teddy-bears' picnic?

4 What do you think happened after the end of the story? What effect do you think the picnic had on Edwin and Deborah's marriage?

Character

5 The story opens with the argument between the two main characters, Edwin and Deborah. What do we learn about them from the way they talk to each other? Who do you sympathize with most, Edwin or Deborah? Why?

6 Both Edwin and Deborah can be described as naive (lacking in life experience) and possibly immature. Which of the two do you think is the most immature? Why?

7 What does Deborah think of Edwin? What does Edwin think of Deborah? Do you think this is a good basis for a marriage?

8 The two main characters have very different interpretations of the main events and aspects of the story. Compare their thoughts and feelings about a) their marriage b) their argument c) the teddy-bears' picnic. What does this tell us about them?

9   What role do the following characters play in the story: Edwin's mother; Deborah's father; Mr Ainley-Foxleton; Angela; the other friends at the picnic? Which of these secondary characters do you think is most important? Why?

10 Why did Edwin nudge Mr Ainley-Foxleton? Do you think he intended to hurt, or even kill, him? What was his immediate reaction to the 'accident'? Why do you think he reacted as he did? How do you think he will feel when he sobers up and realizes what he has done?

Narration

11 Who is telling the story? How do you think the story would have been told differently if the narrator had been a) Deborah b) Edwin? What information would not have been given?

12 Look again at the list of events in exercise 1. In what order are these events described in the story? Is this the same or different to the order in which they actually happened? What effect does this have on the story?

13 There are various points in the story when one of the characters remembers an event from the past (often called a 'flashback'). How many flashbacks are there in the story? Whose memories are being described in each one?

14 The narrator gives a number of different points of view throughout the story. How does he do this? How do you know whose point of view he is giving? Does he ever give an objective, outside view?

Style

Free indirect speech

The narrator often reports the thoughts and feelings of the characters using free indirect speech (often called 'interior monologue'). Indirect speech is a method of reporting what someone else has said without repeating their actual words. For example, at the beginning of the story, Edwin says *'I simply don't believe it'*. We can report these words indirectly as: *Edwin said he didn't believe it*. If we remove the reporting verb (*Edwin said*), we are left with: *He didn't believe it*. This is called 'free indirect speech'.

15 Look at this extract, in which the narrator reports Deborah's thoughts after her argument with Edwin. Complete the spaces in the text below to show her thoughts as direct speech.

They'd had quarrels before. [...] The present quarrel was just the same kind of thing, Deborah knew: Edwin would sit and sulk, she'd wash the dishes up feeling miserable, and he'd probably eat the chop and the broccoli when they were cold. She couldn't blame him.

'I know he'll sit .... ,
I'll .... and he'll ....
when they .... I can't ....'

16 In the extract below Edwin is drinking heavily and thinking about the teddy-bears' picnic. In which sentence do his thoughts begin? Underline the sentences which are **not** free indirect speech.

Edwin discovered that it wasn't easy to drink from a decanter, but he managed it none the less. Anger spurted in him all over again. It seemed incredible that he had married a girl who hadn't properly grown up. None of them had grown up, none of them desired to belong in the adult world, not even the husbands and wives who hadn't been involved in the first place. If Deborah had told him about any of it on that Sunday afternoon when they'd visited this house he wondered, even, if he would have married her.

Find another passage in the story where the author describes one of the characters' thoughts in this way. What effect does this type of interior monologue create?

Metaphors

Metaphors are used to describe a person or thing using language that is normally associated with something very different. The author uses a series of metaphors to describe Edwin's anger and its effect.

17 Look at the extracts below. Notice the verbs the author uses to describe Edwin's anger. In which sentence is the author comparing Edwin's anger to a) a hard object b) mist or fog c) water d) a person?

1 *The anger which had hung about Edwin after the quarrel had never evaporated.*
2 *Further anger had smacked at him when she'd said she hoped he would have a lovely time.*

3 *Anger spurted in him all over again.*
4 *The anger hammered at him now, hurting him almost.*

What is the effect of the metaphor each time? Which do you find most effective? Why?

18 Look again at the paragraph where Edwin enters the Ainley-Foxletons' dining room [page 57]. Underline the verbs in the first three sentences. What are they describing? What effect do they create? Find one more verb in the paragraph that is being used metaphorically (as a metaphor). What does it tell us about Edwin's control of the situation and his own emotions?

19 Read the end of the story again. Notice how short the last paragraph is compared to the previous two. What effect does this create? How does it make you feel at the end of the story?

Guidance to the above literary terms, answer keys to all the exercises and activities, plus a wealth of other reading-practice material, can be found at www.macmillanenglish.com/readers.

The Rough Crossing
by F Scott Fitzgerald

About the author

F Scott Fitzgerald is arguably[1] one of the best-known American writers of the 20th century. He wrote novels, short stories and screenplays for Hollywood films. He is best known for his novels about life in the US 'Jazz Age' in the 1920s.

Francis Scott Key Fitzgerald was born into an upper-middle-class Catholic family in 1896 in St Paul, Minnesota. Fitzgerald was encouraged to write by his teachers at school, and he wrote stories for the school magazine. Even at Princeton University[2], his writing was more important to him than his studies. He joined the army in 1917, and the following summer, when he was at an army camp in Alabama, he met and fell in love with Zelda Sayre. She was the beautiful 18-year-old daughter of rich parents. He desperately wanted to marry her, but Zelda wanted someone who was wealthy and successful.

Determined to win her, Fitzgerald worked hard on his first novel, *This Side of Paradise*. It was published in 1920, sold well, and made Fitzgerald rich. Zelda and he were married, and moved to New York, where he wrote a second novel, *The Beautiful and Damned*. This was also a success, and the Fitzgeralds began to live a life of luxury and excess. Their daughter, Frances, was born in 1921.

Both Fitzgerald and Zelda suffered from health problems, which were made worse by their heavy drinking. In 1925, when they were living in France, *The Great Gatsby*, probably his most famous novel, was published. It showed a darker side of the Jazz Age – restlessness, hard-drinking[3], crime, infidelity and deep unhappiness, as well as the search for excitement, romance, beauty and glamour – but it did not enjoy the same commercial success as his other novels.

Soon afterwards the family returned to the US, where financial worries led to Fitzgerald working for the first time as a Hollywood screenwriter, a job he disliked. The late 1920s were increasingly

1 used for stating your opinion or belief, especially when you think other people may disagree
2 one of the eight prestigious US 'Ivy League' universities
3 spending a lot of time drinking alcohol

unhappy years for the Fitzgeralds, with Scott drinking heavily and Zelda frustrated in her ambitions to become a writer and ballerina.

In 1930, Zelda suffered her first mental breakdown and was diagnosed with schizophrenia. From then until her death in 1948 she spent most of her time in sanatoriums[4] and mental hospitals in Europe and America. Scott's second most famous novel, *Tender is the Night*, was published in 1934. It tells the story of a young American psychiatrist and his marriage to a beautiful schizophrenic patient. In 1937, Fitzgerald began a relationship with Hollywood gossip columnist Sheilah Graham and started writing regularly for Hollywood film studios. He lived with Graham until his death of a heart attack in 1940. He was 44.

Ironically, the novels which were less successful in Fitzgerald's lifetime are now thought to be his best. Several of his books have been made into films, including *The Great Gatsby* and *Tender is the Night*. In addition to his novels, Fitzgerald also wrote over 150 short stories.

About the story

The Rough Crossing was first published in the *Saturday Evening Post* on 8 June 1929, at a time when the *Post*, as it was called, was the most widely circulated weekly magazine in America. It included original works of fiction, and lavish illustrations – which appeared on the cover, in the stories themselves and in the all-important advertising. Some of the illustrations became so popular that they were reproduced as posters or prints, especially those by the world-famous illustrator Norman Rockwell. Publication in the *Post* was enormously important to writers – especially at the start of their careers. Its importance declined only in the late 1950s and 1960s with the arrival of television.

Background information

Passenger liners and the *Titanic*

The story takes place on an ocean super-liner crossing from the USA to Europe. The term *super-liner* was first used in the late 19th century, when ocean-going liners were rapidly increasing in size and speed. In the first half of the 20th century super-liners were the main means of intercontinental travel, and passengers preferred large, fast ships. One

4 large buildings like hospitals where people who have had a serious illness go so that doctors can take care of them while they get better

of the ships mentioned in the story, SS (Steam Ship) *Majestic*, won the famous Blue Riband award for the fastest crossing of the Atlantic in 1891. Their other honeymoon liner, *SS Aquitania*, was built for the Cunard line in 1914 and carried 3230 passengers. Another Cunard super-liner, *RMS* (Royal Mail Ship) *Mauretania*, is also mentioned. It held the speed record for 22 years, from 1907 to 1928.

Because the story is about a *rough* crossing, Fitzgerald is clearly following his readers' fascination with the most famous shipping incident of the 20th century. On 14th April 1912, the largest passenger steamship in the world, the *Titanic*, hit an iceberg shortly before midnight and sank two hours and forty minutes later. Of the 2,223 passengers on board, only just over 700 survived because there were not enough lifeboats for everyone.

The Jazz Age

The story is set in the Jazz Age – the period after World War I and through the 'Roaring Twenties' (the 1920s) – a decade of hope, technological progress and financial prosperity, which ended in severe economic recession[5]. Usually referred to as the Great Depression, this started in the USA in 1929 and lasted until the late 1930s/early 1940s. It was the longest and deepest recession of the 20th century.

Fitzgerald is usually credited with inventing the expression 'the Jazz Age', which he used in the title of one of his short story collections. The term takes its name from jazz music, which during the 1920s gained enormous cultural importance throughout the US. This decade also saw the arrival of the first fast cars, commercial air travel and the telephone.

5 a period when trade and industry are not successful and there is a lot of unemployment

Summary

It may help you to know something about what happens in the story before you read it. Don't worry, this summary does *not* tell you how the story ends!

A celebrity writer, Adrian Smith, and his family, are crossing the Atlantic on an ocean liner on their way to France. Adrian and his wife Eva have been married for seven years. He is now 31, she is 26. At the beginning of the journey they are feeling romantic and want to spend all their time together, but the days pass and slowly they are drawn into the social life aboard the ship.

After two days at sea, the ship is heading towards a storm. Adrian and Eva, beginning to get bored of life at sea, decide to join the other passengers in the smoking room, where they meet a group of young admirers. Adrian is invited to join a tennis tournament on board the ship. He is particularly happy to make the acquaintance of a young woman he noticed when they first boarded the ship and who claims to be a great fan of his. Eva is not so happy, but finds that she, too, has a connection with one of the young men in the group and that they get on well.

Meanwhile, the storm is getting stronger and many of the passengers, including Eva, begin to feel seasick. Adrian, however, is fine, and he joins the young people from the bar to play tennis on deck. As the ship sails further into the storm, the relationship between the husband and wife also becomes more stormy, as Eva grows jealous of her husband and his new friend.

Pre-reading activities

Key vocabulary

This section will help you familiarize yourself with some of the more specific vocabulary used in the story. You may want to use it to help you before you start reading, or as a revision exercise after you have finished the story.

Ocean liners and life on board the ship

1 **Read this description of the boat at the beginning of the story. Notice how the ship is referred to as *she* and *her*, as if it were a woman. Look at the words in bold. Which describe a) people or animals b) parts of the ship or the harbour c) objects or machines d) actions?**

At the beginning of the story the passengers are ready to **board** the liner, which is docked at a **pier** in New York. **Trucks** are carrying luggage and **cargo** to the ship. Porters carry heavy **trunks** up the long **gangplanks** onto the ship whilst **stevedores** and their **cranes** lift heavy boxes on board. Those passengers who are already on board are walking along the **promenade deck**, getting to know the ship, or standing at the **rail**, waving to friends and family below. **Stewards** and **stewardesses** are busy showing passengers to their **cabins** and **staterooms**. In the **purser**'s office names are being checked on lists. On the **bridge**, the captain and his **crew** are getting ready to set off. Sailors are checking that the lifeboats are securely attached to their **stanchions**. Engineers are checking the **wireless** room and the radio **mast**. High above the ship, **gulls** are flying, waiting to accompany the big ship on her journey as she finally sets sail across the Atlantic, her spotless **portholes** shining in the sun.

2 **Read the description in exercise 1 again and match some of the words in bold with their definitions below (1–15).**

1 the part of the ship where the controls are
2 private rooms on a ship for a passenger or one of the people working on the ship (two words)
3 tall machines used for lifting heavy objects
4 the people who work on a ship
5 long boards used for walking on to a ship

6 a tall, metal structure used for sending and receiving radio signals
7 a structure built out from the land over the water and used for getting on and off boats or ships
8 an external part of the ship which runs along the side and where passengers walk and enjoy the view
9 the person who is responsible for the ship's accounts
10 posts that support something
11 people who work on the docks
12 people who work on the ship and look after the passengers (two words)
13 large, strong boxes with a lid, traditionally used for carrying clothes and other things when travelling
14 another word for radio
15 things that are being sent by ship, plane, train or truck

Describing the storm

3 **As the storm grows in intensity, a number of different words are used to describe the weather conditions. Look at the list below. Which of the conditions would you describe as 'extreme'? Have you ever experienced any of these more extreme ones?**

---

damp wet but not actually raining
driving rain rain that falls very fast
driving wind a wind that is blowing strongly
gale a very strong wind
hurricane a violent storm with extremely strong winds and very heavy rain
spray very fine drops of water blown into the air, for example from the sea

---

4 **Verbs of movement play an important part in the description of the ship in the storm. Look at the list below. Which are synonyms of each other? Which are the most violent?**

---

heave to move up and down with large regular movements
hurl to be moved with speed and force in a particular direction
keel over to fall sideways
lurch to move suddenly in a way which is not smooth or controlled
pitch to move up and down suddenly
pound to hit something several times with a lot of force
rock to move backwards and forwards or from side to side in a gentle way
roll to move from side to side
tip to move into a position that is at an angle
toss to make something move up and down or from side to side

Adjectives

5 Here are some of the key adjectives used in the story. Look at the adjectives and their definitions. Which of the adjectives describe a) objects or places b) people and their reactions c) actions or events?

> **dim** not well lit, with very little light
> **dizzy** feeling as if you or the things around you are spinning
> **dreary** making you feel bored or unhappy
> **flushed** looking red because you are hot after physical exercise
> **hazy** not clear because there is smoke, dust or water in the air
> **mournful** making you feel very sad
> **outrageous** very shocking or unreasonable
> **stifling** so hot that it is difficult to breathe
> **swarthy** with dark skin and hair
> **taut** used about a voice or expression to show that someone is nervous or angry
> **touching** making you feel emotional

6 Choose the correct adjective to complete the sentences.

1 'They look **dizzy/dreary/hazy**,' she agreed. 'Let's not get to know anybody, but just stay together.'

2 It was **flushed/outrageous/stifling** for a member of the crew to be seasick.

3 The deference with which she neglected the young men and bent her politeness on him was somehow very **dim/mournful/touching**.

4 The match was over and they had won. **Flushed/Stifling/Swarthy** and hearty, he came up to Eva's chair.

5 'I feel terribly about it.' His voice was **hazy/outrageous/taut** and trembling.

Main themes

Before you read the story, you may want to think about some of its main themes. The questions will help you think about the story as you are reading it for the first time. There is more discussion of the main themes in the *Literary analysis* section after the story.

Class and privilege

The main characters in the story are wealthy people. They are travelling on a luxury liner and have a nurse to look after their children. The liner is full of stewards and stewardesses who are there to look after their every need, and there is a definite class divide between the privileged passengers and the crew.

7 As you read the story think about these questions:

a) How do the main characters treat the crew?
b) To what extent are they aware of the problems the ship and the crew are facing?
c) What is the crew's attitude to their behaviour?

Isolation and disorientation

It is a common literary device to throw a random[6] group of people together in a confined space[7], or a confining situation, and to observe the effect the situation has on their behaviour and the way they interact. In this story the ship is a 'world apart', an artificial community thrown together for the duration of the journey. And the isolation of this world is highlighted by the storm, which distorts[8] reality and leaves the characters to find their way in an unfamiliar world.

8 As you read the story think about the following questions:

a) In what way is the main characters' behaviour on board the ship different from the way they act on land?
b) How does the bad weather affect the passengers, both physically and emotionally?

Atonement

In the heart of the storm, Eva feels that she must make some kind of sacrifice[9] to the storm for her past sins.

9 As you read the story, ask yourself:

a) What does Eva feel guilty about?
b) What sacrifice does she make?

6 chosen or happening without any particular method, pattern or purpose
7 a small space in which you cannot move around easily
8 to change the way that something looks, sounds or behaves so that it becomes strange or difficult to recognize
9 the act of giving up something important or valuable so that you or other people can do or have something else

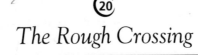

The Rough Crossing

by F Scott Fitzgerald

I

Once on the long, covered piers, you have come into a ghostly country that is no longer Here and not yet There. Especially at night. There is a hazy yellow **vault** full of shouting, echoing voices. There is the rumble of trucks and the clump of trunks, the strident chatter of a crane and the first salt smell of the sea. You hurry through, even though there's time. The past, the continent, is behind you; the future is that glowing mouth in the side of the ship; this dim turbulent alley is too confusedly the present.

Up the gangplank, and the vision of the world adjusts itself, narrows. One is a citizen of a commonwealth smaller than Andorra[10]. One is no longer so sure of anything. Curiously unmoved the men at the purser's desk, cell-like the cabin, disdainful the eyes of voyagers and their friends, solemn the officer who stands on the deserted promenade deck thinking something of his own as he stares at the crowd below. A last odd idea that one didn't really have to come, then the loud, mournful whistles, and the thing – certainly not the boat, but rather a human idea, a frame of mind – pushes forth into the big dark night.

Adrian Smith, one of the celebrities on board – not a very great celebrity, but important enough to be bathed in flashlight by a photographer who had been given his name, but wasn't sure what his subject 'did' – Adrian Smith and his blonde wife, Eva, went up to the promenade deck, passed the melancholy ship's officer, and, finding a quiet aerie[11], put their elbows on the rail.

10 a small country bordered by Spain and France in the Pyrenees (the mountain chain on the Spanish-French border)
11 US: in British English, *eyrie* – a place that is very high and difficult to reach; the nest built by an eagle

'We're going!' he cried presently, and they both laughed in ecstasy. 'We've escaped. They can't get us now.'

'Who?'

He waved his hand vaguely at the civic tiara[12].

'All those people out there. They'll come with their posses[13] and their warrants and list of crimes we've committed, and ring the bell at our door on Park Avenue[14] and ask for the Adrian Smiths, but what ho! the Adrian Smiths and their children and nurse are off for France.'

'You make me think we really have committed crimes.'

'They can't have you,' he said frowning. 'That's one thing they're after me about – they know I haven't got any right to a person like you, and they're furious. That's one reason I'm glad to get away.'

'Darling,' said Eva.

She was twenty-six – five years younger than he. She was something precious to everyone who knew her.

'I like this boat better than the *Majestic* or the *Aquitania*,' she remarked, unfaithful to the ships that had served their honeymoon.

'It's much smaller.'

'But it's very **slick** and it has all those little shops along the corridors. And I think the staterooms are bigger.'

'The people are very formal – did you notice? – as if they thought everyone else was a card sharp[15]. And in about four days half of them will be calling the other half by their first names.'

Four of the people came by now – a quartet of young girls **abreast**, making a circuit of the deck. Their eight eyes swept momentarily towards Adrian and Eva, and then swept automatically back, save for one pair which **lingered** for an

12 a piece of jewellery a woman wears on top of her head on a formal occasion, it is semicircular and looks like a crown. Used here to describe the crowd, which was probably standing in a semicircle

13 *US, informal:* in the past, a group of ordinary men gathered together by a law officer to search for a criminal

14 a wide street in Manhattan, New York City. It is one of the most expensive and prestigious addresses in New York

15 a professional card player who cheats to win money

instant with a little **start**. They belonged to one of the girls in the middle, who was, indeed, the only passenger of the four. She was not more than eighteen – a dark little beauty with the fine crystal gloss over her that, in **brunettes**, takes the place of a blonde's bright glow.

'Now, who's that?' wondered Adrian. 'I've seen her before.'

'She's pretty,' said Eva.

'Yes.' He kept wondering, and Eva **deferred** momentarily **to** his distraction; then, smiling up at him, she drew him back into their privacy.

'Tell me more,' she said.

'About what?'

'About us – what a good time we'll have, and how we'll be much better and happier, and very close always.'

'How could we be any closer?' His arm pulled her to him.

'But I mean never even quarrel any more about silly things. You know, I made up my mind when you gave me my birthday present last week' – her fingers caressed the fine seed pearls at her throat – 'that I'd try never to say a mean thing to you again.'

'You never have, my precious.'

Yet even as he strained her against his side she knew that the moment of **utter** isolation had passed almost before it had begun. His antennae were already out, feeling over this new world.

'Most of the people look rather awful,' he said – 'little and swarthy and ugly. Americans didn't use to look like that.'

'They look dreary,' she agreed. 'Let's not get to know anybody, but just stay together.'

A **gong** was beating now, and stewards were shouting down the decks, 'Visitors **ashore**, please!' and voices rose to a strident chorus. For a while the gangplanks were **thronged**; then they were empty, and the **jostling** crowd behind the barrier waved and called unintelligible things, and kept up a grin of good will. As the stevedores began to work at the ropes a flat-faced, somewhat **befuddled** young man arrived in a great hurry and was assisted up the gangplank by a porter and a taxi driver. The ship having swallowed him as impassively as though he were a missionary for Beirut[16], a low, **portentous** vibration began. The pier with its faces commenced to slide by, and for a moment the boat was just a piece accidentally split off from it; then the faces became remote, voiceless, and the pier was one among many yellow blurs along the water front. Now the harbour flowed swiftly toward the sea.

On a northern parallel of latitude a hurricane was forming and moving south by southeast preceded by a strong west wind. On its course it was destined to **swamp** the *Peter I. Eudin* of Amsterdam, with a crew of sixty-six, to break a **boom** on the largest boat in the world, and to bring **grief** and **want** to the wives of several hundred seamen. This liner, leaving New York Sunday evening, would enter the zone of the storm Tuesday, and of the hurricane late Wednesday night.

II

Tuesday afternoon Adrian and Eva paid their first visit to the smoking-room. This was not in accord with their intentions – they had 'never wanted to see a cocktail again' after leaving America – but they had forgotten the **staccato** loneliness of ships, and all activity centred about the bar. So they went in for just a minute.

It was full. There were those who had been there since luncheon[17], and those who would be there until dinner, not to mention a faithful few who had been there since nine this morning. It was a prosperous **assembly**, taking its recreation at bridge[18], solitaire[19], detective stories, alcohol, argument and love. Up to this point you could have matched it in the club or casino life of any country, but over it all played a repressed nervous energy, a barely disguised impatience that extended to old and young alike. The cruise had begun, and they had

16 the capital city of Lebanon. At the turn of the 20th century Beirut was a centre of missionary activity
17 *formal:* lunch, especially a formal lunch for a lot of people
18 a card game for four players who play in two teams. It was very popular at the beginning of the 20th century and often associated with the upper classes
19 *mainly US:* a card game played by one person, called *patience* in British English

enjoyed the beginning, but the show was not varied enough to last six days, and already they wanted it to be over.

At a table near them Adrian saw the pretty girl who had stared at him on the deck the first night. Again he was fascinated by her loveliness; there was no mist upon the brilliant gloss that **gleamed** through the smoky confusion of the room. He and Eva had decided from the passenger list that she was probably 'Miss Elizabeth D'Amido and maid', and he had heard her called Betsy as he walked past a deck-tennis game. Among the young people with her was the flat-nosed youth who had been 'poured on board', the night of their departure; yesterday he had walked the deck **morosely**, but he was apparently reviving. Miss D'Amido whispered something to him, and he looked over at the Smiths with curious eyes. Adrian was new enough at being a celebrity to turn self-consciously away.

'There's a little roll. Do you feel it?' Eva demanded.

'Perhaps we'd better **split** a pint of champagne.'

While he gave the order a short colloquy[20] was taking place at the other table; presently a young man rose and came over to them.

'Isn't this Mr Adrian Smith?'

'Yes.'

'We wondered if we couldn't put you down for the deck-tennis tournament. We're going to have a deck-tennis tournament.'

'Why –' Adrian hesitated.

'My name's Stacomb,' burst out the young man. 'We all know your – your plays or whatever it is, and all that – and we wondered if you wouldn't like to come over to our table.'

Somewhat **overwhelmed**, Adrian laughed: Mr Stacomb, **glib**, soft, **slouching**, waited; evidently under the impression that he had **delivered himself of** a graceful compliment.

Adrian, understanding that, too, replied: 'Thanks, but perhaps you'd better come over here.'

'We've got a bigger table.'

'But we're older and more – more settled.'

The young man laughed kindly, as if to say, 'That's all right.'

20 *formal, rare*: a dialogue or conference

'Put me down,' said Adrian. 'How much do I owe you?'

'One buck[21]. Call me Stac.'

'Why?' asked Adrian, **startled**.

'It's shorter.'

When he had gone they smiled broadly.

'Heavens,' Eva gasped, 'I believe they are coming over.'

They were. With a great draining of glasses, calling of waiters, shuffling of chairs, three boys and two girls moved to the Smiths' table. If there was any **diffidence**, it was confined to the hosts; for the new additions gathered around them eagerly, eyeing Adrian with respect – too much respect – as if to say: 'This was probably a mistake and won't be amusing, but maybe we'll get something out of it to help us in our after life, like at school[22].'

In a moment Miss D'Amido changed seats with one of the men and placed her radiant self at Adrian's side, looking at him with manifest admiration.

'I fell in love with you the minute I saw you,' she said audibly and without self-consciousness; 'so I'll take all the blame for **butting in**. I've seen your play four times.'

Adrian called a waiter to take their orders.

'You see,' continued Miss D'Amido, 'we're going into a storm, and you might be prostrated[23] the rest of the trip, so I couldn't take any chances.'

He saw that there was no undertone or **innuendo** in what she said, nor the need of any. The words themselves were enough, and the deference with which she neglected the young men and bent her politeness on him was somehow very touching. A little glow went over him; he was having rather more than a pleasant time.

Eva was less entertained; but the flat-nosed young man, whose name was Butterworth, knew people that she did, and that seemed to make the affair less careless and casual. She did not like meeting new people unless they had 'something to contribute', and she was often bored by the great streams

21 US, *informal*: a dollar
22 US, *informal*: a college or university
23 *formal*: extremely upset or ill

of them, of all types and conditions and classes, that passed through Adrian's life. She herself 'had everything' – which is to say that she **was** well **endowed with** talents and with charm – and the mere novelty of people did not seem a sufficient reason for eternally offering everything up to them.

Half an hour later when she rose to go and see the children, she was content that the episode was over. It was colder on deck, with a damp that was almost rain, and there was a perceptible motion. Opening the door of her stateroom she was surprised to find the cabin steward sitting **languidly** on her bed, his head **slumped** upon the upright pillow. He looked at her **listlessly** as she came in, but made no move to get up.

'When you've finished your **nap** you can fetch me a new pillow-case,' she said briskly.

Still the man didn't move. She perceived then that his face was green.

'You can't be seasick in here,' she announced firmly. 'You go and lie down in your own **quarters**.'

'It's me[24] side,' he said faintly. He tried to rise, gave out a little **rasping** sound of pain and sank back again. Eva rang for the stewardess.

A steady pitch, toss, roll had begun in earnest and she felt no sympathy for the steward, but only wanted to get him out as quick as possible. It was outrageous for a member of the crew to be seasick. When the stewardess came in Eva tried to explain this, but now her own head was **whirring**, and throwing herself on the bed, she covered her eyes.

'It's his fault,' she groaned when the man was assisted from the room. 'I was all right and it made me sick to look at him. I wish he'd die.'

In a few minutes Adrian came in.

'Oh, but I'm sick!' she cried.

'Why, you poor baby.' He leaned over and took her in his arms. 'Why didn't you tell me?'

'I was all right upstairs, but there was a steward – Oh, I'm too sick to talk.'

24 *non-standard spoken English*: my

'You'd better have dinner in bed.'

'Dinner! Oh, my heavens!'

He waited **solicitously**, but she wanted to hear his voice, to have it **drown out** the complaining sound of the beams.

'Where've you been?'

'Helping to sign up people for the tournament.'

'Will they have it if it's like this? Because if they do I'll just lose for you.'

He didn't answer; opening her eyes, she saw that he was frowning.

'I didn't know you were going in the doubles,' he said.

'Why, that's the only fun.'

'I told the D'Amido girl I'd play with her.'

'Oh.'

'I didn't think. You know I'd much rather play with you.'

'Why didn't you, then?' she asked coolly.

'It never occurred to me.'

She remembered that on their honeymoon they had been in the finals and won a prize. Years passed. But Adrian never frowned in this regretful way unless he felt a little guilty. He stumbled about, getting his dinner clothes out of the trunk, and she shut her eyes.

When a particular violent lurch startled her awake again he was dressed and tying his tie. He looked healthy and fresh, and his eyes were bright.

'Well, how about it?' he inquired. 'Can you make it, or no?'

'No.'

'Can I do anything for you before I go?'

'Where are you going?'

'Meeting those kids in the bar. Can I do anything for you?'

'No.'

'Darling, I hate to leave you like this.'

'Don't be silly. I just want to sleep.'

That solicitous frown – when she knew he was crazy to be out and away from the close cabin. She was glad when the door closed. The thing to do was to sleep, sleep.

Up – down – sideways. Hey there, not so far! Pull her round the corner there! Now roll her, right – left – Crea-eak![25] Wrench! Swoop!

Some hours later Eva was dimly conscious of Adrian bending over her. She wanted him to put his arms around her and draw her up out of this dizzy **lethargy**, but by the time she was fully awake the cabin was empty. He had looked in and gone. When she awoke next the cabin was dark and he was in bed.

The morning was fresh and cool, and the sea was just enough calmer to make Eva think she could get up. They breakfasted in the cabin and with Adrian's help she **accomplished** an unsatisfactory **makeshift** toilet[26] and they went up on the boat deck. The tennis tournament had already begun and was furnishing action for a dozen amateur movie cameras, but the majority of passengers were represented by lifeless **bundles** in deck chairs beside untasted trays.

Adrian and Miss D'Amido played their first match. She was **deft** and graceful; **blatantly** well. There was even more warmth behind her ivory skin than there had been the day before. The strolling first officer stopped and talked to her; half a dozen men whom she couldn't have known three days ago called her Betsy. She was already the pretty girl of the voyage, the cynosure[27] of starved ship's eyes.

But after a while Eva preferred to watch the gulls in the wireless masts and the slow slide of the **roll-top** sky. Most of the passengers looked silly with their movie cameras that they had all rushed to get and now didn't know what to use for, but the sailors painting the lifeboat stanchions were quiet and beaten and sympathetic, and probably wished, as she did, that the voyage was over.

Butterworth sat down on the deck beside her chair.

'They're operating on one of the stewards this morning. Must be terrible in this sea.'

25 non-standard spelling used to illustrate the sound
26 *formal*: the process of washing and getting dressed
27 *formal*: someone or something that is a centre of attention and admiration, often because they are beautiful or brilliant

'Operating? What for?' she asked listlessly.

'Appendicitis[28]. They have to operate now because we're going into worse weather. That's why they're having the ship's party tonight.'

'Oh, the poor man!' she cried, realizing it must be her steward.

Adrian was **showing off** now by being very courteous and thoughtful in the game.

'Sorry. Did you hurt yourself? … No, it was my fault … You better put on your coat right away, partner, or you'll catch cold.'

The match was over and they had won. Flushed and **hearty**, he came up to Eva's chair.

'How do you feel?'

'Terrible.'

'Winners are buying a drink in the bar,' he said apologetically.

'I'm coming, too,' Eva said, but an immediate dizziness made her sink back in her chair.

'You'd better stay here. I'll send you up something.'

She felt that his public manner had hardened towards her slightly.

'You'll come back?'

'Oh, right away.'

She was alone on the boat deck, save for a solitary ship's officer who slanted **obliquely** as he paced the bridge. When the cocktail arrived she forced herself to drink it, and felt better. Trying to distract her mind with pleasant things, she reached back to the **sanguine** talks that she and Adrian had had before sailing: There was the little villa in Brittany[29], the children learning French – that was all she could think of now – the little villa in Brittany, the children learning French – so she repeated the words over and over to herself until they became as meaningless as the wide white sky. The why of their being here had suddenly **eluded** her; she felt unmotivated, accidental, and she wanted Adrian to come back quick, all responsive and tender, to reassure her. It was in the hope that there was some

28 *medical*: an illness in which your appendix becomes infected and has to be removed in a medical operation

29 a region in the north-west of France

secret of graceful living, some real compensation for the lost, careless confidence of twenty-one, that they were going to spend a year in France.

The day passed darkly, with fewer people around and a wet sky falling. Suddenly it was five o'clock, and they were all in the bar again, and Mr Butterworth was telling her about his past. She took a good deal of champagne, but she was seasick dimly through it, as if the illness was her soul trying to struggle up through some thickening **incrustation** of abnormal life.

'You're my idea of a Greek goddess, physically,' Butterworth was saying.

It was pleasant to be Mr Butterworth's idea of a Greek goddess physically, but where was Adrian? He and Miss D'Amido had gone out on a forward deck to feel the spray. Eva heard herself promising to get out her colours and paint the Eiffel Tower[30] on Butterworth's shirt front for the party tonight.

When Adrian and Betsy D'Amido, **soaked** with spray, opened the door with difficulty against the driving wind and came into the now-covered security of the promenade deck, they stopped and turned toward each other.

'Well?' she said. But he only stood with his back to the rail, looking at her, afraid to speak. She was silent, too, because she wanted him to be first; so for a moment nothing happened. Then she made a step towards him, and he took her in his arms and kissed her forehead.

'You're just sorry for me, that's all.' She began to cry a little. 'You're just being kind.'

'I feel terribly about it.' His voice was taut and trembling.

'Then kiss me.'

The deck was empty. He bent over her swiftly.

'No, really kiss me.'

He could not remember when anything had felt so young and fresh as her lips. The rain lay, like tears shed for him, upon the softly shining **porcelain** cheeks. She was all new and immaculate, and her eyes were wild.

'I love you,' she whispered. 'I can't help loving you, can I?

30 a famous landmark in Paris

When I first saw you – oh, not on the boat, but over a year ago – Grace Heally took me to a **rehearsal** and suddenly you jumped up in the second row and began telling them what to do. I wrote you a letter and tore it up.'

'We've got to go.'

She was weeping as they walked along the deck. Once more, **imprudently**, she held up her face to him at the door of her cabin. His blood was beating through him in wild tumult as he walked on to the bar.

He was thankful that Eva scarcely seemed to notice him or to know that he had been gone. After a moment he pretended an interest in what she was doing.

'What's that?'

'She's painting the Eiffel Tower on my shirt front for tonight,' explained Butterworth.

'There,' Eva laid away her brush and wiped her hands. 'How's that?'

'A *chef-d'oeuvre*[31].'

Her eyes swept around the watching group, lingered casually upon Adrian.

'You're wet. Go and change.'

'You come too.'

'I want another champagne cocktail.'

'You've had enough. It's time to dress for the party.'

Unwilling she closed her paints and preceded him.

'Stacomb's got a table for nine,' he remarked as they walked along the corridor.

'The younger set,' she said with unnecessary bitterness. 'Oh, the younger set. And you just having the time of your life – with a child.'

They had a long discussion in the cabin, unpleasant on her part and evasive on his, which ended when the ship gave a sudden gigantic heave, and Eva, the edge worn off her champagne, felt ill again. There was nothing to do but to have a cocktail in the cabin, and after that they decided to go to the party – she

31 *French*: masterpiece

believed him now, or she didn't care.

Adrian was ready first – he never wore **fancy dress**.

'I'll go on up. Don't be long.'

'Wait for me, please; it's rocking so.'

He sat down on a bed, concealing his impatience.

'You don't mind waiting, do you? I don't want to parade up there all alone.'

She was taking a **tuck** in an oriental costume rented from the barber.

'Ships make people feel crazy,' she said. 'I think they're awful.'

'Yes,' he muttered absently.

'When it gets very bad I pretend I'm in the top of a tree, rocking **to and fro**. But finally I get pretending everything, and finally I have to pretend I'm sane when I know I'm not.'

'If you get thinking that way you will go crazy.'

'Look, Adrian.' She held up the string of pearls before clasping them on. 'Aren't they lovely?'

In Adrian's impatience she seemed to move around the cabin like a figure in a slow-motion picture[32]. After a moment he demanded:

'Are you going to be long? It's stifling in here.'

'You go on!' she fired up.

'I don't want –'

'Go on, please! You just make me nervous trying to hurry me.'

With a show of reluctance he left her. After a moment's hesitation he went down a **flight** to a deck below and knocked at a door.

'Betsy.'

'Just a minute.'

She came out in the corridor attired in a red pea-jacket[33] and trousers borrowed from the elevator boy.

'Do elevator boys have fleas?' she demanded. 'I've got everything in the world on under this as a precaution.'

'I had to see you,' he said quickly.

'Careful,' she whispered. 'Mrs Worden, who's supposed to be

32 *mainly US:* film

33 a heavy jacket, made of wool, that was originally worn by sailors in Europe

chaperoning me, is across the way. She's sick.'

'I'm sick for you.'

They kissed suddenly, **clung** close together in the narrow corridor, swaying to and fro with the motion of the ship.

'Don't go away,' she murmured.

'I've got to. I've –'

Her youth seemed to flow into him, bearing him up into a delicate romantic ecstasy that **transcended** passion. He couldn't relinquish it; he had discovered something that he had thought was lost with his own youth forever. As he walked along the passage he knew that he had stopped thinking, no longer dared to think.

He met Eva going into the bar.

'Where've you been?' she asked with a strained smile.

'To see about the table.'

She was lovely; her cool distinction conquered the **trite** costume and filled him with a resurgence of approval and pride. They sat down at a table.

The gale was rising hour by hour and the mere traversing of a passage had become a rough matter. In every stateroom trunks were **lashed** to the washstands, and the *Vestris* disaster[34] was being reviewed in detail by nervous ladies, tossing, ill and wretched, upon their beds. In the smoking-room a stout gentleman had been hurled backward and suffered a badly cut head; and now the lighter chairs and tables were stacked and roped against the wall.

The crowd who had donned[35] fancy dress and were dining together had swollen to about sixteen. The only remaining qualification for membership was the ability to reach the smoking-room. They ranged from a Groton-Harvard[36] lawyer to an ungrammatical broker they had nicknamed Gyp the Blood[37], but distinctions had disappeared; for the moment they

34 in 1928 the ocean liner SS *Vestris* ran into a severe storm while on a voyage from New Jersey to Barbados. 65 passengers and 45 members of the crew died

35 *mainly literary*: put on clothes

36 who had been to Groton, an elite private school, and Harvard University

37 Harry Horowitz (1889–1914), better known as *Gyp the Blood*, was the leader of a notorious New York City gang in the early 20th century

were samurai, chosen from several hundred for their triumphant resistance to the storm.

The gala dinner, overhung **sardonically** with lanterns and streamers, was interrupted by great communal slides across the room, **precipitate** retirements and spilled wine, while the ship roared and complained that under the panoply[38] of a palace it was a ship after all. Upstairs afterward a dozen couples tried to dance, shuffling and galloping here and there in a crazy fandango[39], **thrust** around fantastically by a will alien to their own. In view of the condition of tortured hundreds below, there grew to be something indecent about it like a revel[40] in a house of mourning, and presently there was an egress[41] of the ever-**dwindling** survivors towards the bar.

As the evening passed, Eva's feeling of unreality increased. Adrian had disappeared – presumably with Miss D'Amido – and her mind, distorted by illness and champagne, began to enlarge upon the fact; annoyance changed slowly to dark and brooding anger, grief to desperation. She had never tried to **bind** Adrian, never needed to – for they were serious people, with all sorts of mutual interests, and satisfied with each other – but this was a **breach** of the contract, this was cruel. How could he think that she didn't know?

It seemed several hours later that he leaned over her chair in the bar where she was giving some woman an impassioned lecture upon babies, and said:

'Eva, we'd better turn in[42].'

Her lip curled. 'So that you can leave me there and then come back to your eighteen-year –'

'Be quiet.'

'I won't come to bed.'

'Very well. Good night.'

More time passed and the people at the table changed. The

---

38 *formal:* a large and impressive display
39 a fast dance from Spain
40 *mainly literary:* a lively and noisy party or celebration, especially where people sing, dance and drink alcohol
41 *very formal:* the action of leaving a place
42 *informal, old-fashioned:* to go to bed at night

stewards wanted to close up the room, and thinking of Adrian – her Adrian – off somewhere saying **tender** things to someone fresh and lovely, Eva began to cry.

'But he's gone to bed,' her last attendants assured her. 'We saw him go.'

She shook her head. She knew better. Adrian was lost. The long seven-year dream was broken. Probably she was punished for something she had done; as this thought occurred to her the shrieking **timbers** overhead began to mutter that she had guessed at last. This was for the selfishness to her mother, who hadn't wanted her to marry Adrian; for all the sins and omissions of her life. She stood up, saying she must go out and get some air.

The deck was dark and **drenched** with wind and rain. The ship pounded through valleys, fleeing from black mountains of water that roared towards it. Looking out at the night, Eva saw that there was no chance for them unless she could make **atonement**, propitiate[43] the storm. It was Adrian's love that was demanded of her. Deliberately she unclasped her pearl necklace, lifted it to her lips – for she knew that with it went the freshest, fairest part of her life – and **flung** it out into the gale.

III

When Adrian awoke it was lunchtime, but he knew that some heavier sound than the bugle[44] had called him up from his deep sleep. Then he realized that the trunk had broken loose from its lashings and was being thrown back and forth between a wardrobe and Eva's bed. With an exclamation he jumped up, but she was unharmed – still in costume and stretched out in deep sleep. When the steward had helped him secure the trunk, Eva opened a single eye.

'How are you?' he demanded, sitting on the side of her bed.

She closed the eye, opened it again.

'We're in a hurricane now,' he told her. 'The steward says it's the worst he's seen in twenty years.'

43 *formal:* to try to stop someone from being angry with you by doing something to please them

44 a musical instrument sometimes used to show that an activity is about to begin or end

'My head,' she muttered. 'Hold my head.'

'How?'

'In front. My eyes are going out. I think I'm dying.'

'Nonsense. Do you want the doctor?'

She gave a funny little gasp that frightened him; he rang and sent the steward for the doctor.

The young doctor was pale and tired. There was a stubble of beard upon his face. He **bowed curtly** as he came in and, turning to Adrian, said with **scant** ceremony:

'What's the matter?'

'My wife doesn't feel well.'

'Well, what is it you want – a bromide[45]?'

A little annoyed by his shortness, Adrian said: 'You'd better examine her and see what she needs.'

'She needs a bromide,' said the doctor. 'I've given orders that she is not to have any more to drink on this ship.'

'Why not?' demanded Adrian in astonishment.

'Don't you know what happened last night?'

'Why, no, I was asleep.'

'Mrs Smith wandered around the boat for an hour, not knowing what she was doing. A sailor was sent to follow her, and then the medical stewardess tried to get her to bed, and your wife insulted her.'

'Oh, my heavens!' cried Eva faintly.

'The nurse and I had both been up all night with Steward Carton, who died this morning.' He picked up his case. 'I'll send down a bromide for Mrs Smith. Good-bye.'

For a few minutes there was silence in the cabin. Then Adrian put his arm around her quickly.

'Never mind,' he said. 'We'll straighten it out.'

'I remember now.' Her voice was an **awed** whisper. 'My pearls. I threw them overboard.'

'Threw them overboard!'

'Then I began looking for you.'

'But I was here in bed.'

'I didn't believe it; I thought you were with that girl.'

45 a drug to make people calm or help them to sleep

'She collapsed during dinner. I was taking a nap down here.'

Frowning, he rang the bell and asked the steward for luncheon and a bottle of beer.

'Sorry, but we can't serve any beer to your cabin, sir.'

When he went out Adrian exploded: 'This is an **outrage**. You were simply crazy from that storm and they can't be so **high-handed**. I'll see the captain.'

'Isn't that awful?' Eva murmured. 'The poor man died.'

She turned over and began to sob into her pillow. There was a knock at the door.

'Can I come in?'

The assiduous[46] Mr Butterworth, surprisingly healthy and immaculate, came into the crazily tipping cabin.

'Well, how's the mystic?' he demanded of Eva. 'Do you remember praying to **the elements** in the bar last night?'

'I don't want to remember anything about last night.'

They told him about the stewardess, and with the telling the situation lightened; they all laughed together.

'I'm going to get you some beer to have with your luncheon,' Butterworth said. 'You ought to get up on deck.'

'Don't go,' Eva said. 'You look so cheerful and nice.'

'Just for ten minutes.'

When he had gone, Adrian rang for two baths.

'The thing is to put on our best clothes and walk proudly three times around the deck,' he said.

'Yes.' After a moment she added **abstractedly**: 'I like that young man. He was awfully nice to me last night when you'd disappeared.'

The bath steward appeared with the information that bathing was too dangerous today. They were in the midst of the wildest hurricane on the North Atlantic in ten years; there were two broken arms this morning from attempts to take baths. An elderly lady had been thrown down a staircase and was not expected to live. Furthermore, they had received the SOS[47] signal from several boats this morning.

46 *formal:* hard-working and thorough
47 Save Our Souls, a radio signal used for calling for help, especially by a ship or a plane

'Will we go to help them?'

'They're all behind us, sir, so we have to leave them to the *Mauretania*. If we tried to turn in this sea the portholes would be smashed.'

This **array** of **calamities** minimized their own troubles. Having eaten a sort of luncheon and drunk the beer provided by Butterworth, they dressed and went on deck.

Despite the fact that it was only possible to progress step by step, holding on to rope or rail, more people were **abroad** than on the day before. Fear had driven them from their cabins, where the trunks bumped and the waves pounded the portholes, and they awaited momentarily the call to the boats. Indeed, as Adrian and Eva stood on the **transverse** deck above the second class, there was a bugle call, followed by a gathering of stewards and stewardesses on the deck below. But the boat was sound: it had outlasted one of its cargo – Steward James Carton was being buried at sea.

It was very British and sad. There were the rows of stiff, disciplined men and women standing in the driving rain, and there was a shape covered by the flag of the Empire that lived by the sea[48]. The chief purser read the service, a hymn was sung, the body slid off into the hurricane. With Eva's burst of wild weeping for this humble end, some last string snapped within her. Now she really didn't care. She responded eagerly when Butterworth suggested that he get some champagne to their cabin. Her mood worried Adrian; she wasn't used to so much drinking and he wondered what he ought to do. At his suggestion that they sleep instead, she merely laughed, and the bromide the doctor had sent stood untouched on the washstand. Pretending to listen to the insipidities[49] of several Mr Stacombs, he watched her; to his surprise and discomfort she seemed on intimate and even sentimental terms with Butterworth and he wondered if this was a form of revenge for his attention to Betsy D'Amido.

The cabin was full of smoke, the voices went on incessantly, the suspension of activity, the waiting for the storm's end, was

48 the British Empire
49 *formal*: boring or dull things that a person says

getting on his nerves. They had been at sea only four days; it was like a year.

The two Mr Stacombs left finally, but Butterworth remained. Eva was urging him to go for another bottle of champagne.

'We've had enough,' objected Adrian. 'We ought to go to bed.'

'I won't go to bed!' she burst out. 'You must be crazy! You play around all you want, and then, when I find somebody I – I like, you want to put me to bed.'

'You're **hysterical**.'

'On the contrary, I've never been so sane.'

'I think you'd better leave us, Butterworth,' Adrian said. 'Eva doesn't know what she's saying.'

'He won't go, I won't let him go.' She clasped Butterworth's hand passionately. 'He's the only person that's been half decent to me.'

'You'd better go, Butterworth,' repeated Adrian.

The young man looked at him uncertainly.

'It seems to me you're being unjust to your wife,' he ventured.

'My wife isn't herself.'

'That's no reason for bullying her.'

Adrian lost his temper. 'You get out of here!' he cried.

The two men looked at each other for a moment in silence. Then Butterworth turned to Eva, said, 'I'll be back later,' and left the cabin.

'Eva, you've got to pull yourself together,' said Adrian when the door closed.

She didn't answer, looked at him from **sullen**, half-closed eyes.

'I'll order dinner here for us both and then we'll try to get some sleep.'

'I want to go up and send a wireless[50].'

'Who to?'

'Some Paris lawyer. I want a divorce.'

In spite of his annoyance, he laughed. 'Don't be silly.'

50 *old-fashioned*: a radio message

'Then I want to see the children.'

'Well, go and see them. I'll order dinner.'

He waited for her in the cabin twenty minutes. Then impatiently he opened the door across the corridor; the nurse told him that Mrs Smith had not been there.

With a sudden prescience[51] of disaster he ran upstairs, glanced in the bar, the salons, even knocked at Butterworth's door. Then a quick round of the decks, feeling his way through the black spray and rain. A sailor stopped him at a network of ropes.

'Orders are no one goes by, sir. A wave has gone over the wireless room.'

'Have you seen a lady?'

'There was a young lady here –' He stopped and glanced around. 'Hello, she's gone.'

'She went up the stairs!' Adrian said anxiously. 'Up to the wireless room!'

The sailor ran up to the boat deck; stumbling and **slipping**, Adrian followed. As he cleared the protected sides of the companionway[52], a tremendous body struck the boat a staggering blow and, as she keeled over to an angle of forty-five degrees, he was thrown in a helpless roll down the drenched deck, to bring up dizzy and **bruised** against a stanchion.

'Eva!' he called. His voice was soundless in the black storm. Against the faint light of the wireless-room window he saw the sailor making his way forward.

'Eva!'

The wind blew him like a sail up against a lifeboat. Then there was another shuddering crash, and high over his head, over the very boat, he saw a gigantic, glittering white wave, and in the split second that it balanced there he became conscious of Eva, standing beside a ventilator[53] twenty feet away. Pushing out from the stanchion, he **lunged** desperately toward her, just as the wave broke with a smashing roar. For a moment the rushing water was five feet deep, sweeping with enormous force towards

51 *formal:* the condition of knowing or behaving as if you know what will happen in the future

52 a stair or ladder within the hull of a vessel; the space occupied by this stair or ladder

53 a machine that brings fresh air into a room or building and moves it around

the side, and then a human body was washed against him, and frantically he clutched it and was swept with it back towards the rail. He felt his body bump against it, but desperately he held on to his **burden**; then, as the ship rocked slowly back, the two of them, still joined by his fierce grip, were rolled out exhausted on the wet planks. For a moment he knew no more.

IV

Two days later, as the boat train moved tranquilly south toward Paris, Adrian tried to persuade his children to look out the window at the Norman[54] countryside.

'It's beautiful,' he assured them. 'All the little farms like toys. Why, in heaven's name, won't you look?'

'I like the boat better,' said Estelle.

Her parents exchanged an infanticidal[55] glance.

'The boat is still rocking for me,' Eva said with a **shiver**. 'Is it for you?'

'No. Somehow, it all seems a long way off. Even the passengers looked unfamiliar going through the **customs**.'

'Most of them hadn't appeared above ground[56] before.'

He hesitated. 'By the way, I cashed Butterworth's cheque for him.'

'You're a fool. You'll never see the money again.'

'He must have needed it pretty badly or he would not have come to me.'

A pale and **wan** girl, passing along the corridor, recognized them and put her head through the doorway.

'How do you feel?'

'Awful.'

'Me, too,' agreed Miss D'Amido. 'I'm **vainly** hoping my **fiancé** will recognize me at the Gare du Nord[57]. Do you know two waves went over the wireless room?'

---

54 adjective used to describe things in and from Normandy, a region in the north of France
55 adjective for *infanticide*, the crime of killing a baby or very young child. Used comically here
56 on the deck of the ship, rather than in the cabins on the lower decks
57 a train station in Paris

'So we heard,' Adrian answered dryly.

She passed gracefully along the corridor and out of their life.

'The real truth is that none of it happened,' said Adrian after a moment. 'It was a nightmare – an incredibly awful nightmare.'

'Then, where are my pearls?'

'Darling, there are better pearls in Paris. I'll take the responsibility for those pearls. My real belief is that you saved the boat.'

'Adrian, let's never get to know anyone else, but just stay together always – just we two.'

He tucked her arm under his and they sat close. 'Who do you suppose those Adrian Smiths on the boat were?' he demanded. 'It certainly wasn't me.'

'Nor me.'

'It was two other people,' he said, nodding to himself. 'There are so many Smiths in this world.'

Post-reading activities

Understanding the story

Use these questions to help you check that you have understood the story.

I

1   What is being described in the first two paragraphs?
2   Why does a photographer take a photo of Adrian?
3   Where do the couple go after the photo has been taken?
4   What are they looking down at?
5   Are the crimes Adrian talks about real or imaginary? Are the police really looking for the couple?
6   Where are they going to and who are they travelling with?
7   Why does Eva prefer this boat to the others she mentions?
8   Why does the girl look at Adrian?
9   What does Adrian think about the girl?
10 In what way do Adrian and Eva react differently to the passengers on the boat?
11 How do they know the boat is about to leave?
12 How do you know that the storm is going to be a big one?
13 In how many days is the boat expected to meet the storm?

II

14 How many days have passed since the beginning of the story?
15 Where do Adrian and Eva decide to go? Why?
16 How long do they plan to stay there?
17 Why does Stacomb come over to Adrian and Eva's table?
18 How does Adrian feel about the young people? How does Eva feel about them?
19 Why does Eva go to her cabin?
20 What is her reaction when she sees the steward on her bed?
21 How does Eva feel when Adrian comes to the cabin?
22 Why does Adrian feel guilty as he leaves the cabin?
23 What are the passengers doing on the deck the next morning?
24 How do Adrian and Eva join in?
25 Why doesn't Eva go down to the bar after the tournament has finished?
26 What kind of mood is she in?
27 Later that evening Eva is in the bar with Mr Butterworth. What are they talking about?

28 Where is Adrian?
29 Why is Betsy crying?
30 How does Betsy make Adrian feel?
31 What does Eva accuse Adrian of?
32 What do you think Adrian and Eva argue about in the cabin?
33 How does the boat make Eva feel?
34 Where does Adrian go when he leaves the cabin?
35 How does the weather affect the party and the other passengers on the ship?
36 In what way does the party seem unreal?
37 What is Eva worried about?
38 Why does she throw her pearls into the sea?

III

39 What wakes Adrian and Eva up the next morning?
40 Why is the doctor so unfriendly and unhelpful?
41 What do we find out about what Eva did the night before? Who tells us?
42 How does Butterworth help Adrian and Eva feel better?
43 What has been happening while the Adrian Smiths have been asleep?
44 Why are the crew gathered on the deck?
45 What effect does the gathering have on Eva?
46 Why does Adrian ask Butterworth to leave the cabin?
47 What is Butterworth's reaction? And Eva's?
48 Where does Eva say she's going? Where does she really go? Why?
49 Why does Adrian go looking for her?
50 Where does he find Eva?
51 What brings them back together?

IV

52 Where are they now?
53 How have Adrian and Eva's attitudes changed?
54 How do they feel about what happened on the ship?
55 How do they feel about each other now?

Language study

Present participle clauses

Throughout the story Fitzgerald uses present participle clauses to add detail to his descriptions of people, objects and actions.

Form

A present participle clause usually starts with a present participle (verb + -ing). It does not contain a subject or an auxiliary verb:

Frowning, he rang the bell.

To form the negative add *not* before the present participle:

*Mrs Smith wandered around the boat for an hour, **not knowing what she was doing**.*

The present participle clause can also include:

a) an object: *The sailors **painting the lifeboat stanchions** were quiet.*
b) an adverb: *She was surprised to find the cabin steward **sitting languidly** on her bed.*
c) a prepositional phrase: ***Smiling up at him**, she drew him back into their privacy.*

1 **Look at the five example sentences above. What is the subject of each of the clauses in bold?**

Position

Present participle clauses can be placed:

a) at the beginning of a sentence
b) after a noun or noun phrase
c) after the main clause

2 **Find examples of the three positions (a–c) in the example sentences above.**

Use

The present participle clause replaces a full clause.

Smiling up at him, she drew him back into their privacy. (= **She smiled up at him** and *she drew him back into their privacy*.)

Or a relative clause:

The sailors **painting the lifeboat stanchions** *were quiet*. (= *The sailors* **who were painting the lifeboat stanchions** *were quiet*.)

You can only use a present participle clause to replace a relative clause when the relative pronoun (*who*, *which*, etc) is the subject of the verb.

3 **Rewrite the present participle clauses in bold in the sentences below as either full clauses or relative clauses.**

1 *Opening the door of her stateroom she was surprised to find the cabin steward* **sitting languidly on her bed**.
2 *He met Eva* **going into the bar**.
3 *A pale and wan girl,* **passing along the corridor**, *recognized them*.
4 *He became conscious of Eva,* **standing beside a ventilator**.

Present participle clauses are used to:
a) show that two actions happened at the same time
b) give more information about a person or object
c) combine two sentences

Note: They are *not* used to describe the main action or event in a sentence.

4 **Find examples of uses a–c in the sentences in exercise 3.**

5 **Look again at the sentences in 3. What is the main event in each one?**

6 **Rewrite the following sentences, or pairs of sentences, using a present participle clause. Then check your answers in the story.**

1 Eva was dimly conscious of Adrian. He was bending over her. [Page 88]

_____

2 Eva looked out at the night. Eva saw that there was no chance for them. [Page 95]

_____

3 It was only possible to progress step by step, and you had to hold on to the rope or rail. [Page 98]

_____

4   There were the rows of stiff, disciplined men and women who were standing in the driving rain. [Page 98]

5   He saw the sailor as he made his way forward. [Page 100]

6   He pushed out from the stanchion and he lunged desperately toward her. [Page 100]

Homonyms

Homonyms are words that have the same spelling and pronunciation but different meanings:

> But I **mean** never even quarrel any more about silly things. (mean = want to say)
>
> I'd try never to say a **mean** thing to you again. (mean = not nice)

We can also think of these groups of meanings as being **multiple meanings** of the same word.

7   **Look at the words in the box. How many meanings can you think of for each one?**

back	close	mind	right	rock	save

8   **For each group (A–F), choose one of the words from the box to complete all three sentences.**

A

1   The thing – certainly not the boat, but rather a human idea, a frame of .... – pushes forth into the big dark night.

2   'Never .... ,' he said. 'We'll straighten it out.'

3   You don't .... waiting, do you?

B

1   'The boat is still .... ing for me,' Eva said with a shiver. 'Is it for you?'

2   The boat hit a .... under the water and sank swiftly to the bottom of the sea.

3   He played bass guitar in a .... band.

C

1 They had had to .... up for years to pay for their luxury cruise holiday.

2 My real belief is that you ....d the boat.

3 She was alone on the boat deck, ... for a solitary ship's officer.

D

1 Butterworth turned to Eva, said, 'I'll be .... later,' and left the cabin.

2 He stood with his .... to the rail, looking at her, afraid to speak.

3 He realized that the trunk had broken loose from its lashings and was being thrown .... and forth between a wardrobe and Eva's bed.

E

1 He tucked her arm under his and they sat .... 'Who do you suppose those Adrian Smiths on the boat were?' he demanded. 'It certainly wasn't me.'

2 She knew he was crazy to be out and away from the .... cabin.

3 'Tell me more,' she said.
'About what?'
'About us – what a good time we'll have, and how we'll be much better and happier, and very .... always.'

F

1 'They can't have you,' he said frowning. 'That's one thing they're after me about – they know I haven't got any .... to a person like you, and they're furious. That's one reason I'm glad to get away.'

2 Up – down – sideways. Hey there, not so far! Pull her round the corner there! Now roll her, ... – left – Crea-eak! Wrench! Swoop!

3 'It's his fault,' she groaned when the man was assisted from the room. 'I was all .... and it made me sick to look at him. I wish he'd die.'

Literary analysis

Plot

1 Look at the series of events below. How much time passes between each event? Which one event do you think is the most important? Why?

   a) The passengers board the ship.
   b) The ship sets sail.
   c) Adrian and Eva first enter the smoking room.
   d) Adrian plays in the deck-tennis tournament.
   e) They both go to the fancy dress party.
   f) Eva throws her pearls into the sea.
   g) Adrian finds Eva near the wireless room.
   h) They travel by train to Paris.

2 Look at this second list of background events. When did they take place? Add these events to the list in exercise 1. Which one event from this second list do you think is most important for the story?

   i) The ship entered the storm.
   j) The steward was taken ill.
   k) The storm reached hurricane force.
   l) Various passengers were injured, one very seriously.
   m) The steward died.
   n) The steward was buried.
   o) Two waves hit the wireless room.

3 The story begins on land and finishes on land. What effect does this create? Are you interested in finding out what happens next? Why/Why not? Do you think the experience of the journey will change the way Adrian and Eva feel about each other?

Character

4 What do you know about the two main characters? What part of society do they represent? To what extent do you think they might be typical of their class?

5 Both Adrian and Eva are guilty of being selfish, and ignoring the feelings and needs of other people. Think of examples from the story. Which of the two characters do you think is the most self-centred?

6 Eva talks about the storm driving her crazy. Think of examples of her behaviour that could be described as 'mad'. What other factors, apart from the storm, influence her behaviour?

7 Why was Adrian attracted to Betsy? How did she make him feel? What does this tell us about Adrian? Do you think Betsy was really in love with Adrian? Why/Why not?

8 Why did Eva enjoy Butterworth's company so much? What did he represent for her?

9 Do you think any of the characters grow or change during the story, or do they simply return to their normal lives as if nothing has happened?

Narration

10 Who tells the story? In what way would the story have been different if it had been told by a) Adrian b) Eva c) Betsy, Butterworth or one of the other passengers d) the ship's doctor or one of the stewards?

11 Are the main events described in chronological order (the order in which they actually happened)? Is there any reference to events or situations before the story? If so, why are these events or situations described?

12 How do we find out what Eva did after the fancy dress party? What does this tell us about her frame of mind?

13 Who comments on the story, and the journey, at the beginning? Who comments at the end? What do you think is the main subject of the story? What does the story tell us about a) journeys b) people's behaviour in extreme situations?

Style

14 Look at the opening paragraphs again. What are they describing? What is your overall impression of the docks and the ship?

15 Notice the words used to describe the ship: *a commonwealth smaller than Andorra, the thing, a human idea, a frame of mind*. What effect does this language create for you? What is the author telling us about the ship?

16 Look again at the first paragraph. What sounds and smells are described? Notice the repetition in the structure within the sentences:
…no longer Here and not yet There.

...the rumble of trucks and the clump of trunks, the strident chatter of a crane and the first salt smell of the sea.

The past, the continent, is behind you; the future is that glowing mouth in the side of the ship; this dim turbulent alley is too confusedly the present.

What effect do these descriptions create? How do the passengers feel as they board the ship?

17 Look again at the second paragraph. Underline all the adjectives. What do they have in common? What is the overall impression? Look again at the adjectives in the fourth sentence. What is each adjective describing? What is unusual about their position? What effect does this create?

18 The author uses dialogue throughout the story to explore the relationships between the various characters: between Adrian and Eva, between Adrian and Betsy, and also between Eva and the crew. Look at the first dialogue between Adrian and Eva [page 81]. What does this tell us about them?

19 Look at the dialogue between Eva and the crew, when she finds the sick steward in the cabin [page 86]. What does this tell us about her, and the theme of class and privilege?

20 The story opens with a dense, detailed description. It closes with dialogue. Look again at this closing dialogue. What is the atmosphere at the end of the story? How does it contrast with the atmosphere at the beginning? What does this tell us about a) the journey b) the story?

Guidance to the above literary terms, answer keys to all the exercises and activities, plus a wealth of other reading-practice material, can be found at www.macmillanenglish.com/readers.

Lamb to the Slaughter

by Roald Dahl

About the author

Roald Dahl was a British/Norwegian novelist, short story writer and writer of TV plays. He is best known for his children's books, *Charlie and the Chocolate Factory, Fantastic Mr Fox* and *Danny the Champion of the World*, all of which have been made into successful children's films. He is also well known for his *Tales of the Unexpected*, short stories with a twist in their tail (an unexpected ending).

Roald Dahl was born in 1916 in Cardiff, Wales, the son of wealthy Norwegians. When Roald was three, his father died. But his mother stayed in Britain so that her children could go to school there. However, they spent their long summer holidays with her in Norway. It was there that she encouraged Dahl's fascination with insects and birds, and with witches and trolls[1]. Dahl immortalized[2] his mother as the grandmother in his children's story *The Witches* (1983).

Dahl was educated in a number of different schools and sent away to a boarding school at the age of nine. He was not happy at school as he was not particularly academic, but he excelled at sports, and when he finished school at 18, instead of going to university he set off on an expedition to Newfoundland with the Public Schools Exploring Society.

In 1934 he started work for the Shell oil company in Tanganyika[3]. When World War II started in 1939, he joined the Royal Air Force in Kenya. In 1940 he was badly injured when his plane ran out of fuel and he had to crash-land in the Libyan desert. After seven months in hospital he took part in desperate air defences over Athens and the Peloponnese in southern Greece. His short story *Katina* (1944) describes the horrors of an air raid[4] as experienced by civilians.

In 1942 he was sent to Washington; and from 1943 to 1945 he

1 very ugly creatures in old Scandinavian stories that live in caves and are either very small or very tall
2 immortalize (verb): to make someone or something famous for a very long time, for example by writing about them or by painting them
3 a former territory in East Africa, now part of the nation of Tanzania
4 an attack in which one or more planes drop bombs on a place

worked for the American intelligence service, together with author Ian Fleming, the creator of James Bond. He also became a frequent guest of Eleanor and President Franklin D Roosevelt at the White House following the success of his story *The Gremlins* (1943), about a tribe of goblins that cause problems with RAF aircraft.

After the war Dahl was one of the first authors to write stories of black comedy[5]. These were published in prestigious American magazines like *The New Yorker* and *Harper's*, before appearing in book form in *Someone Like You* (1953) and *Kiss Kiss* (1960). In 1953 he married film star Patricia Neal. They had five children – one son, who suffered brain damage in an accident in New York, and four daughters, one of whom died at the age of seven. In 1965, when his wife became dangerously ill while pregnant with their fifth child, he used his enormous energy and intelligence to help her re-learn to walk and talk. He had earlier been active in the development of the Wade-Dahl-Till valve to help relieve his son's hydrocephalus (also known as 'water on the brain'), which resulted from the accident.

In 1961, Dahl published his first book for children, *James and the Giant Peach*, in which a young boy is orphaned when his parents are eaten by an escaped rhinoceros. Anti-adult, rude and sometimes cruel, the story was an immediate popular success, as was *Charlie and the Chocolate Factory* (1964).

In 1983 Dahl divorced Patricia Neal and married her friend, Felicity d'Abreu Crosland. They lived at Gipsy House in the Buckinghamshire countryside west of London. There he enjoyed chocolate, fine wines and orchids, and looked after his 100 budgerigars[6] that flew wild around the garden. The house is now a Dahl museum in celebration of one of the most popular children's writer ever. He died in 1990 and was given a Viking-style funeral near Oxford – buried with him were chocolates, some excellent French wine, HB[7] pencils, his snooker cues[8] and a power saw[9].

5   stories, plays or films that deal in a humorous way with unpleasant aspects of life
    such as illness and death. Black comedy became an extremely important feature of
    popular British culture in the 1960s
6   small bright blue, green or yellow birds often kept as pets. Also known as 'budgies'
7   the grade for a standard writing pencil
8   long thin sticks that you use for hitting the ball in games such as snooker and pool
9   an electrical tool used for cutting wood or metal

About the story

After being rejected by *The New Yorker* magazine, *Lamb to the Slaughter* was first published in *Harper's Magazine* in September 1953, and in a collection of short stories called *Someone Like You* (also 1953). It was later adapted successfully for an episode of *Alfred Hitchcock Presents* – a TV series featuring dramas, thrillers and mysteries – which was originally broadcast in 1958.

Background information

Lamb to the slaughter

Slaughter is the killing of animals, usually for their meat. Lambs are often used as symbols of innocence. The expression 'like a lamb to the slaughter' is used to describe someone who is approaching danger or a dangerous situation without complaining or arguing, usually because they don't know what is going to happen and are therefore not frightened.

Housewives in the 1950s

In the Britain, Ireland and America of the late 1940s and 1950s, married middle-class women usually didn't work, or stopped working when they had children. Instead, many of them were good housewives and provided the kind of warm, clean and comfortable home that we find in *Lamb to the Slaughter*. Like the perfect housewife of the period, Mary Maloney has a welcoming drink ready for her hard-working husband on his return home from work.

Leg of lamb

Roast meat – traditionally lamb, beef or pork – served with potatoes and two or three other vegetables, is a traditional British main meal. The most popular cut of lamb is the leg, which is roasted in the oven.

Capital punishment

At the time the story was written, the death penalty (capital punishment) was still in force for murder in the UK. It was abolished[10] in 1969 in Great Britain and in 1973 in Northern Ireland.

---

10 abolish (verb): to officially get rid of a law, system, practice, etc

Summary

It may help you to know something about what happens in the story before you read it. Don't worry, this summary does *not* tell you how the story ends!

Mary Maloney sits at home sewing peacefully and waiting for her husband to come back from work. She is six months pregnant. When he arrives, she watches him enjoy his first whisky of the evening in silence. When he finishes the second half of it quickly, she thinks he must be very tired and offers to get him another glass so that he doesn't have to get up after such a long day. He is a senior policeman – and detective, as we find out later – but he still has to walk about all day. She then wonders how else she can help. Does he want his slippers? Does he want some cheese? Does he want to eat in, rather than go out as usual on Thursday evening? Does he want lamb or pork?

He then tells her to sit down as he has something to say to her. She listens quietly to what he has to say. She is so shocked that she doesn't know what to believe, or what to do. So she decides to prepare dinner and goes downstairs to get some meat from the freezer...

Pre-reading activities

Key vocabulary

This section will help you familiarize yourself with some of the more specific vocabulary used in the story. You may want to use it to help you before you start reading, or as a revision exercise after you have finished the story.

Describing the Maloneys' home

1 The Maloneys live in a comfortable, middle-class home. In the box on the next page are some of the features of the house and furniture mentioned in the story. Look at the words and their definitions and answer the following questions.

1 Which would you expect to find in a living room?
2 Which would you find outside the house?
3 Which are not part of your own home?

> **back door** a door at the back or side of a building, not the main entrance
> **cabinet** a piece of furniture with doors and shelves or drawers that is used for storing things or for showing attractive objects
> **cellar** a room under a building, below the level of the ground, usually used for storing things
> **closet** (*mainly US*) a small room or space built into a wall for storing things such as clothes or sheets
> **front door** the main door at the front of a house
> **gravel** small pieces of stone used for making paths or roads
> **mantel** (*US*) in British English, *mantelpiece* – a shelf above the opening of a fireplace
> **sideboard** a large piece of furniture that has shelves and cupboards for storing dishes, glasses, etc
> **table lamp** a small light that is designed to stand on a table
> **Thermos bucket** an object that keeps liquids cold or hot
> **vase** a container for cut flowers

Police and police procedures

2 **Patrick Maloney is a police officer and the story contains a lot of vocabulary describing the police and their procedures. Look at these short extracts and match the words in bold with their definitions (a–f).**

1 *Two policemen walked in. She knew them both – she knew nearly all the men at that **precinct**.*

2 *A police photographer arrived and took pictures, and a man who knew about **fingerprints**.*

3 *After a while, the photographer and the doctor departed and two other men came in and took the **corpse** away on a **stretcher**.*

4 *They were looking for the **weapon**. The murderer may have taken it with him, but on the other hand he may've thrown it away or hidden it somewhere on the **premises**.*

a) a dead body
b) marks that you leave on something when you touch it
c) a local police station (*mainly US*)
d) buildings and/or land (*formal*)
e) a type of bed used for carrying someone who is injured, ill or dead
f) an object that can be used to hurt people or damage property

Large heavy objects

3 The police are interested in finding a heavy, blunt (not pointed) object. Look at the three examples they give in the story. Which do you think they are least likely to find in the Maloneys' home?

club a heavy object with a flat or round end, used as a weapon, or to play golf
sledgehammer a long heavy hammer that you swing with both hands, usually used in construction
spanner a metal tool that you use for turning small pieces of metal called nuts to make them tighter

Adjectives

4 Look at these key adjectives from the story and their definitions. Which of the adjectives are a) positive b) negative?

bewildered not really understanding and not certain what to do
blissful giving you great pleasure
dazed unable to think clearly because you are shocked, upset, tired or have been hit on the head
exasperated extremely annoyed and impatient because things are not happening in the way that you want
placid peaceful, not experiencing or showing excitement
tranquil calm and still

5 In the following sentences, replace the word/s in bold with an adjective from exercise 4.

1 She lowered herself back slowly into the chair, watching him all the time with those large, **confused** eyes.

2 For her, this was always a **very happy** time of day.

3 She sat very still through it all, watching him with a kind of **stunned** horror.

4 The mouth was soft, and the eyes, with their new **happy, unmoved** look, seemed larger, darker than before.

5 The drop of the head as she bent over her sewing was curiously **quiet**.

6 The four men searching the rooms seemed to be growing weary, a trifle **frustrated**.

Main themes

Before you read the story, you may want to think about some of its main themes. The questions will help you think about the story as you are reading it for the first time. There is more discussion of the main themes in the *Literary analysis* section after the story.

Marital roles

The main characters in the story are a married couple, and the story starts with a fairly typical scene in their lives.

6 As you read the story, ask yourself:

a) What are Mary and Patrick's roles in their marriage?
b) Do you think the two characters are comfortable in their marital roles? Why/Why not?

Revenge

Patrick Maloney breaks some bad news to his wife. The main part of the story describes her reaction to this bad news.

7 As you read the story think about the following questions:

a) Are you surprised by Mary's reaction?
b) Do you think she planned to do what she did?
c) Why did she do it?

Lying

A main theme in the story is the search for truth and how easy it can be to lie.

8 As you read the story consider these questions:

a) In what way has Patrick been lying to Mary?
b) Does Mary find it difficult to lie? Why/Why not?
c) Are her lies convincing? Why/Why not?

Lamb to the Slaughter

by Roald Dahl

The room was warm and clean, the curtains **drawn**, the two table lamps **alight** – hers and the one by the empty chair opposite. On the sideboard behind her, two tall glasses, soda water, whisky. Fresh ice cubes in the Thermos bucket.

Mary Maloney was waiting for her husband to come home from work.

Now and again she would glance up at the clock but without anxiety, merely to please herself with the thought that each minute gone by made it nearer the time when he would come. There was a slow smiling **air** about her, and about everything she did. The drop of the head as she bent over her sewing was curiously tranquil. Her skin – for this was her sixth month with child[11] – had acquired a wonderful **translucent** quality, the mouth was soft, and the eyes, with their new placid look, seemed larger, darker than before.

When the clock said ten minutes to five, she began to listen, and a few moments later, punctually as always, she heard the tyres on the gravel outside, and the car door **slamming**, the footsteps passing the window, the key turning in the lock. She laid aside her sewing, stood up, and went forward to kiss him as he came in.

'Hullo, darling,' she said.

'Hullo,' he answered.

She took his coat and hung it in the closet. Then she walked over and made the drinks, a strongish one for him, a weak one for herself and soon she was back again in her chair with the sewing, and he in the other, opposite, holding the tall glass with both his hands, rocking it so the ice cubes **tinkled** against the side.

11 *old-fashioned*: pregnant

For her, this was always a blissful time of day. She knew he didn't want to speak much until the first drink was finished, and she, on her side, was content to sit quietly, enjoying his company after the long hours alone in the house. She loved to **luxuriate** in the presence of this man, and to feel – almost as a sunbather feels the sun – that warm male glow that came out of him to her when they were alone together. She loved him for the way he sat **loosely** in a chair, for the way he came in a door, or moved slowly across the room with long strides. She loved the **intent**, far look in his eyes when they rested on her, the funny shape of the mouth, and especially the way he remained silent about his tiredness, sitting still with himself until the whisky had taken some of it away.

'Tired, darling?'

'Yes,' he said. 'I'm tired.' And as he spoke, he did an unusual thing. He lifted his glass and drained it in one swallow although there was still half of it, at least half of it, left. She wasn't really watching him but she knew what he had done because she heard the ice cubes falling back against the bottom of the empty glass when he lowered his arm. He paused a moment, leaning forward in his chair, then he got up and went slowly over to fetch himself another.

'I'll get it!' she cried, jumping up.

'Sit down,' he said.

When he came back, she noticed that the new drink was dark **amber** with the quantity of whisky in it.

'Darling, shall I get your slippers?'

'No.'

She watched him as he began to **sip** the dark yellow drink, and she could see little oily **swirls** in the liquid because it was so strong.

'I think it's a shame,' she said, 'that when a policeman gets to be as senior as you, they keep him walking about on his feet all day long.'

He didn't answer, so she bent her head again and went on with her sewing; but each time he lifted the drink to his lips, she heard the ice cubes **clinking** against the side of the glass.

'Darling,' she said. 'Would you like me to get you some cheese? I haven't made any supper because it's Thursday.'

'No,' he said.

'If you're too tired to eat out,' she went on, 'it's still not too late. There's plenty of meat and stuff in the freezer, and you can have it right here and not even move out of the chair.'

Her eyes waited on him for an answer, a smile, a little nod, but he made no sign.

'Anyway,' she went on, 'I'll get you some cheese and **crackers** first.'

'I don't want it,' he said.

She moved uneasily in her chair, the large eyes still watching his face. 'But you *must* have supper. I can easily do it here. I'd like to do it. We can have lamb **chops**. Or pork. Anything you want. Everything's in the freezer.'

'Forget it,' he said.

'But, darling, you *must* eat! I'll fix it anyway, and then you can have it or not, as you like.'

She stood up and placed her sewing on the table by the lamp.

'Sit down,' he said. 'Just for a minute, sit down.'

It wasn't till then that she began to get frightened.

'Go on,' he said. 'Sit down.'

She lowered herself back slowly into the chair, watching him all the time with those large, bewildered eyes. He had finished the second drink and was staring down in the glass frowning.

'Listen,' he said, 'I've got something to tell you.'

'What is it, darling? What's the matter?'

He had become absolutely **motionless**, and he kept his head down so that the light from the lamp beside him fell across the upper part of his face, leaving the chin and mouth in shadow. She noticed there was a little muscle moving near the corner of his left eye.

'This is going to be a bit of a shock to you, I'm afraid,' he said. 'But I've thought about it a good deal and I've decided the only thing to do is tell you right away. I hope you won't blame me too much.'

And he told her. It didn't take long, four or five minutes at most, and she sat very still through it all, watching him with a kind of dazed horror as he went further and further away from her with each word.

'So there it is,' he added. 'And I know it's kind of a bad time to be telling you, but there simply wasn't any other way. Of course I'll give you money and see you're looked after. But there needn't really be any fuss. I hope not anyway. It wouldn't be very good for my job.'

Her first instinct was not to believe any of it, to reject it all. It occurred to her that perhaps he hadn't even spoken, that she herself had imagined the whole thing. Maybe, if she **went about her business** and acted as though she hadn't been listening, then later, when she sort of woke up again, she might find none of it had ever happened.

'I'll get the supper,' she managed to whisper, and this time he didn't stop her.

When she walked across the room she couldn't feel her feet touching the floor. She couldn't feel anything at all – except a slight **nausea** and a desire to vomit. Everything was automatic now – down the stairs to the cellar, the light switch, the **deep freeze**, the hand inside the cabinet taking hold of the first object it met. She lifted it out, and looked at it. It was wrapped in paper, so she took off the paper and looked at it again.

A leg of lamb.

All right then, they would have lamb for supper. She carried it upstairs, holding the thin bone-end of it with both her hands, and as she went through the living-room, she saw him standing over by the window with his back to her, and she stopped.

'For God's sake,' he said, hearing her, but not turning round. 'Don't make supper for me. I'm going out.'

At that point, Mary Maloney simply walked up behind him and without any pause she swung the big frozen leg of lamb high in the air and brought it down as hard as she could on the back of his head.

She might just as well have hit him with a steel club.

She stepped back a **pace**, waiting, and the funny thing was that he remained standing there for at least four or five seconds, gently swaying. Then he crashed to the carpet.

The violence of the crash, the noise, the small table overturning, helped bring her out of the shock. She came out slowly, feeling cold and surprised, and she stood for a while blinking at the body, still holding the ridiculous piece of meat tight with both hands.

All right, she told herself. So I've killed him.

It was extraordinary, now, how clear her mind became **all of a sudden**. She began thinking very fast. As the wife of a detective, she knew quite well what the penalty would be. That was fine. It made no difference to her. In fact, it would be a relief. On the other hand, what about the child? What were the laws about murderers with unborn children? Did they kill them both – mother and child? Or did they wait until the tenth month? What did they do?

Mary Maloney didn't know. And she certainly wasn't prepared to take a chance.

She carried the meat into the kitchen, placed it in a pan, turned the oven on high, and **shoved** it inside. Then she washed her hands and ran upstairs to the bedroom. She sat down before the mirror, tidied her face, **touched up** her lips and face. She tried a smile. It came out rather peculiar. She tried again.

'Hullo, Sam,' she said brightly, aloud.

The voice sounded peculiar too.

'I want some potatoes please, Sam. Yes, and I think a can of peas.'

That was better. Both the smile and the voice were coming out better now. She rehearsed it several times more. Then she ran downstairs, took her coat, went out the back door, down the garden, into the street.

It wasn't six o'clock yet and the lights were still on in the grocery shop.

'Hullo, Sam,' she said brightly, smiling at the man behind the counter.

'Why, good evening, Mrs Maloney. How're *you*?'

'I want some potatoes please, Sam. Yes, and I think a can of peas.'

The man turned and reached up behind him on the shelf for the peas.

'Patrick's decided he's tired and doesn't want to eat out tonight,' she told him. 'We usually go out Thursdays, you know, and now he's caught me without any vegetables in the house.'

'Then how about meat, Mrs Maloney?'

'No, I've got meat, thanks. I got a nice leg of lamb from the freezer.'

'Oh.'

'I don't much like cooking it frozen, Sam, but I'm taking a chance on it this time. You think it'll be all right?'

'Personally,' the grocer said, 'I don't believe it makes any difference. You want these Idaho[12] potatoes?'

'Oh yes, that'll be fine. Two of those.'

'Anything else?' The grocer **cocked** his head on one side, looking at her pleasantly. 'How about afterwards? What you going to give him for afterwards?'

'Well – what would you suggest, Sam?'

The man glanced around his shop. 'How about a nice big slice of **cheesecake**? I know he likes that.'

'Perfect,' she said. 'He loves it.'

And when it was all wrapped and she had paid, she put on her brightest smile and said, 'Thank you, Sam. Goodnight.'

'Goodnight, Mrs Maloney. And thank *you*.'

And now, she told herself as she hurried back, all she was doing now, she was returning home to her husband and he was waiting for his supper; and she must cook it good, and make it as tasty as possible because the poor man was tired; and if, when she entered the house, she happened to find anything unusual, or tragic, or terrible, then naturally it would be a shock and she'd become frantic with grief and horror. Mind you, she wasn't *expecting* to find anything. She was just going home with the vegetables. Mrs Patrick Maloney going home with the

12 a state in the north-west of the USA

vegetables on Thursday evening to cook supper for her husband.

That's the way, she told herself. Do everything right and natural. Keep things absolutely natural and there'll be no need for any acting at all.

Therefore, when she entered the kitchen by the back door, she was **humming** a little tune to herself and smiling.

'Patrick!' she called. 'How are you, darling?'

She put the **parcel** down on the table and went through into the living-room; and when she saw him lying there on the floor with his legs doubled up and one arm twisted back underneath his body, it really was rather a shock. All the old love and **longing** for him **welled up** inside her, and she ran over to him, knelt down beside him, and began to **cry her heart out**. It was easy. No acting was necessary.

A few minutes later she got up and went to the phone. She knew the number of the police station, and when the man at the other end answered, she cried to him, 'Quick! Come quick! Patrick's dead!'

'Who's speaking?'

'Mrs Maloney. Mrs Patrick Maloney.'

'You mean Patrick Maloney's dead?'

'I think so,' she sobbed. 'He's lying on the floor and I think he's dead.'

'Be right over,' the man said.

The car came over quickly, and when she opened the front door, two policemen walked in. She knew them both – she knew nearly all the men at that precinct – and she fell right into Jack Noonan's arms, weeping hysterically. He put her gently into a chair, then went over to join the other one, who was called O'Malley, kneeling by the body.

'Is he dead?' she cried.

'I'm afraid he is. What happened?'

Briefly, she told her story about going out to the grocer and coming back to find him on the floor. While she was talking, crying and talking, Noonan discovered a small patch of **congealed** blood on the dead man's head. He showed it to

O'Malley who got up at once and hurried to the phone.

Soon, other men began to come into the house. First a doctor, then two detectives, one of whom she knew by name. Later, a police photographer arrived and took pictures, and a man who knew about fingerprints. There was a great deal of whispering and muttering beside the corpse, and the detectives kept asking her a lot of questions. But they always treated her kindly. She told her story again, this time right from the beginning, when Patrick had come in, and she was sewing, and he was tired, so tired he hadn't wanted to go out for supper. She told how she'd put the meat in the oven – 'it's there now, cooking' – and how she'd slipped out to the grocer for vegetables, and come back to find him lying on the floor.

'Which grocer?' one of the detectives asked.

She told him, and he turned and whispered something to the other detective who immediately went outside into the street.

In fifteen minutes he was back with a page of notes, and there was more whispering, and through her sobbing she heard a few of the whispered phrases – '…acted quite normal…very cheerful… wanted to give him a good supper…peas…cheesecake… impossible that she…'

After a while, the photographer and the doctor departed and two other men came in and took the corpse away on a stretcher. Then the fingerprint man went away. The two detectives remained, and so did the two policemen. They were exceptionally nice to her, and Jack Noonan asked if she wouldn't rather go somewhere else, to her sister's house perhaps, or to his own wife who would take care of her and **put her up** for the night.

No, she said. She didn't feel she could move even a **yard** at the moment. Would they mind awfully if she stayed just where she was until she felt better? She didn't feel too good at the moment, she really didn't.

Then hadn't she better lie down on the bed? Jack Noonan asked.

No, she said, she'd like to stay right where she was, in this chair. A little later perhaps, when she felt better, she would move.

So they left her there while they went about their business, searching the house. Occasionally one of the detectives asked her another question. Sometimes Jack Noonan spoke to her gently as he passed by. Her husband, he told her, had been killed by a blow on the back of the head administered[13] with a heavy **blunt instrument**, almost certainly a large piece of metal. They were looking for the weapon. The murderer may have taken it with him, but on the other hand he may've thrown it away or hidden it somewhere on the premises.

'It's the old story,' he said. 'Get the weapon, and you've got the man.'

Later, one of the detectives came up and sat beside her. Did she know, he asked, of anything in the house that could've been used as the weapon? Would she mind having a look around to see if anything was missing – a very big spanner for example, or a heavy metal vase.

They didn't have any heavy metal vases, she said.

'Or a big spanner?'

She didn't think they had a big spanner. But there might be some things like that in the garage.

The search went on. She knew that there were other policemen in the garden all around the house. She could hear their footsteps on the gravel outside, and sometimes she saw the flash of a torch through a **chink** in the curtains. It began to get late, nearly nine she noticed by the clock on the mantel. The four men searching the rooms seemed to be growing weary, **a trifle** exasperated.

'Jack,' she said, the next time Sergeant Noonan went by. 'Would you mind giving me a drink?'

'Sure I'll give you a drink. You mean this whisky?'

'Yes, please. But just a small one. It might make me feel better.' He handed her the glass.

'Why don't you have one yourself,' she said. 'You must be

13 *formal*: given, carried out

awfully tired. Please do. You've been very good to me.'

'Well,' he answered. 'It's not strictly allowed, but I might take just a drop to keep me going.'

One by one the others came in and were persuaded to take a little **nip** of whisky. They stood around rather awkwardly with the drinks in their hands, uncomfortable in her presence, trying to say **consoling** things to her. Sergeant Noonan wandered into the kitchen, came out quickly and said, 'Look, Mrs Maloney. You know that oven of yours is still on, and the meat still inside.'

'Oh *dear* me!' she cried. 'So it is!'

'I better turn it off for you, hadn't I?'

'Will you do that, Jack? Thank you so much.'

When the sergeant returned the second time, she looked at him with her large, dark tearful eyes. 'Jack Noonan,' she said.

'Yes?'

'Would you do me a small favour – you and these others?'

'We can try, Mrs Maloney.'

'Well,' she said. 'Here you all are, and good friends of dear Patrick's too, and helping to catch the man who killed him. You must be terribly hungry by now because it's long past your supper time, and I know Patrick would never forgive me, God bless his soul, if I allowed you to remain in his house without offering you decent **hospitality**. Why don't you eat up that lamb that's in the oven? It'll be cooked just right by now.'

'Wouldn't dream of it,' Sergeant Noonan said.

'Please,' she **begged**. 'Please eat it. Personally I couldn't touch a thing, certainly not what's been in the house when he was here. But it's all right for you. It'd be a favour to me if you'd eat it up. Then you can go on with your work again afterwards.'

There was a good deal of hesitating among the four policemen, but they were clearly hungry, and in the end they were persuaded to go into the kitchen and help themselves. The woman stayed where she was, listening to them through the open door, and she could hear them speaking among themselves, their voices thick and **sloppy** because their mouths were full of meat.

'Have some more, Charlie?'

'No. Better not finish it.'

'She *wants* us to finish it. She said so. Be doing her a favour.'

'Okay then. Give me some more.'

'That's a hell of a[14] big club the guy must've used to hit poor Patrick,' one of them was saying. 'The doc says his skull was smashed all to pieces just like from a sledge-hammer.'

'That's why it ought to be easy to find.'

'Exactly what I say.'

'Whoever done it, they're not going to be carrying a thing like that around with them longer than they need.'

One of them **belched**.

'Personally, I think it's right here on the premises.'

'Probably right **under our very noses**. What you think, Jack?'

And in the other room, Mary Maloney began to giggle.

---

14 US, *informal*, *spoken*: in British English, *a/one hell of a* – used for emphasizing what you are saying

Post-reading activities

Understanding the story

1   **Use these questions to help you check that you have understood the story.**

Coming home

1   What time is it at the beginning of the story?
2   What preparations has Mary made for her husband when he comes home?
3   Is she looking forward to seeing him?
4   What kind of mood is she in?
5   How does she know her husband is home?
6   What is the difference in the way Mary and Patrick say hello to each other?
7   Who pours the first drinks?

Breaking the news

8   What is unusual about the way Patrick drinks his first whisky?
9   How is his second drink different from the first?
10 What does Mary offer to get for her husband? How does he respond?
11 When does Mary start to worry about her husband's behaviour? Why?
12 What does he tell her?
13 What is her immediate reaction?
14 Why does she get up?
15 How does she feel?
16 Why does she take the leg of lamb upstairs?
17 What is Patrick's reaction when he hears Mary coming back up from the cellar?
18 Why does she hit him?

Alibi

19 How does she feel after her initial shock?
20 What is the first thing that now comes into her mind? Why does this worry her?
21 What does she now do with the leg of lamb? Why?
22 Why does she talk to herself in the mirror?
23 Who is Sam?
24 What exactly does Mary tell Sam? Why?
25 What does she buy? Why?

26 What is Mary thinking as she walks home?
27 Why does she call to her husband when she gets home?
28 What is her reaction when she sees Patrick again? Does this
    reaction seem strange to you?

The police arrive

29 Who is Jack Noonan? And O'Malley?
30 How do the policemen treat Mary?
31 Do you think they suspect her?
32 What does Mary do while the policemen search the house?
33 How does Jack think Patrick was killed? With what?
34 How does Jack think they'll solve the crime?
35 What are the policemen looking for?
36 Why does Mary invite the policemen to eat the lamb?
37 Why doesn't Mary want to eat the lamb?
38 Why does Mary start to laugh?

Language study

Speculating – modal verbs

When the police arrive at the Maloneys' home they speculate about
how Patrick Maloney died and who might have killed him. Notice how
they use the modal verbs *may*, *could* and *must*:

> *The murderer **may have taken** it with him.*
> *But on the other hand he **may've thrown** it away.*
> *Did she know … of anything … that **could've been** used as the weapon?*
> *That's a hell of a big club the guy **must've used** to hit poor Patrick.*

Form

The following modal verb forms are used to speculate about the past:

modal verb (*not*) + *have* + past participle
*Someone **must have hit** him with a heavy object.*

You can also use passive and continuous forms after *have*:
Passive: *He **must have been hit** over the head with a large, metal object.*
Continuous: *She **must have been shopping** at the time.*

Use

Here are some more possible speculations about Patrick Maloney's murder:

a) *She can't have killed him – she looked too cheerful.*

b) *It might have been a burglar who broke into the house.*

1 Underline the modal verbs in sentences (a) and (b) above. Which of these modal verbs has the same meaning as *may have*? Which is the opposite of *must have*?

2 Match the modal verbs in the box with their meanings (1–3) below. Note: There may be more than one answer for some of the meanings.

> can't have   could have   may have   might have   must have

1 I am sure that this is what happened. It seems to be the only logical deduction.   must have

2 I am sure that this did not happen.   *can't have*

3 I think that this is a possible or logical explanation, but not the only one.   may have , might have , could

3 Rewrite the following speculations using *can't have, may have* or *must have.*

1 I'm sure Patrick Maloney was killed by a man.   must

2 I'm sure it wasn't a woman.   must

3 It's possible that the murder weapon was a tool of some sort.   may

4 I'm sure the murderer didn't take the weapon away from the scene of the crime.   *can't*

5 I'm sure Mary Maloney was telling the truth.   must

6 I suppose it's possible that she was acting.   may

Multiple-clause sentences

The actions and situations in the story are very closely observed, and often described in great detail. This often means a lot of long, complex sentences made up of a number of different clauses.

4 Look at this sentence from the story, which contains five clauses. These clauses can be expressed as five simpler sentences, starting with the phrases in 1–5 below. Complete the simple sentences 1–5.

Her skin – for this was her sixth month with child – had acquired a wonderful translucent quality, the mouth was soft, and the eyes, with their new placid look, seemed larger, darker than before.

1 She was in her sixth ....
2 Her skin had acquired ....
3 Her mouth ....
4 Her eyes had a new ....
5 They seemed ....

5 Answer these questions about the original sentence and five simple sentences in exercise 4:

1 What words and phrases have been added to the simple sentences?
2 What words have been omitted?
3 What is the effect of using the one, long sentence in the story? What would be the effect of using the five simpler sentences instead?

6 Look at the sentences below. Can you combine them to make one, complex sentence, like the one in exercise 4?

1 He paused a moment.
2 He leant forward in his chair.
3 He got up.
4 He went slowly across the room.
5 He fetched himself another glass of whisky.

When you have finished, compare your sentence to the one in the story [page 120].

7 Find two more complex, multi-clause sentences in the story. What are they describing? What is the effect of using one, long complex sentence in each case?

Literary analysis

Plot

1   The plot of the story is relatively simple. There are not many key events. Make a list of these events in the order they happen. Which two events do you think are the most important? Why?

2   How long does the action in the story take? How is the passing of time measured? Which moments are described in most detail? Why?

3   What is the significance of the scene in the shop? What does it tell us about Mary?

4   Why don't the policemen suspect Mary? How can we tell this from the way they talk about the murder?

5   Did you expect the twist at the end of the story? Do you think Mary planned for the policemen to eat the leg of lamb from the moment she murdered her husband?

6   What do you think happens next, after the story has finished?

Character

7   What do you know about Mary and Patrick? Which character is described most fully? How would you describe their marriage at the beginning of the story? Do you think Mary is happy? Why/Why not?

8   Does Mary love Patrick? Do you think Patrick loves Mary? Are you surprised by her actions? Why/Why not?

9   Do you think Mary is a good actress? At what points in the story do you think she is deliberately acting? Is she convincing? Why/Why not?

10   How does our image of Mary develop throughout the story? In what way does she seem different at the end of the story?

11   Do you think Mary regrets what she's done? How do you think this will affect her in the future?

Narration

12   Who tells the story? Whose point of view is most important? How is this point of view communicated to the reader?

13   If the story had been narrated from the point of view of one of the policemen, how would it have been different? What information would we lose?

14 Are the actions described in the order they actually happened? What effect does this have on the story?

15 Most of the key events in the story are described through dialogue. What effect does this create? In which scene do you think it is most effective?

Style

16 The plot is very simple and the story fairly straightforward, but it is very carefully observed in all its smallest details. Look at the opening paragraph. What do we learn about the scene and the people we are going to meet in it? What is the atmosphere in this opening paragraph and what details help to create it?

17 From the moment he comes home, Patrick's movements are followed and described in great detail. Why? What effect does this create?

18 Notice the images used when the narrator describes Mary's feelings towards her husband:

She loved to luxuriate in the presence of this man, and to feel – almost as a sunbather feels the sun – that warm male glow that came out of him to her when they were alone together.

What does she compare her husband to? What is the significance of this comparison? What physical feelings does the description make you think of? What does this tell us about Mary's attitude to her husband?

19 Dahl uses short paragraphs of one or two sentences to comment on what is happening. Find the following sentences in the story. How do these sentences help to change the pace and focus of the story?

A leg of lamb.
She might just as well have hit him with a steel club.
All right, she told herself. So I've killed him.
Mary Maloney didn't know. And she certainly wasn't prepared to take a chance.
And in the other room, Mary Maloney began to giggle.

Guidance to the above literary terms, answer keys to all the exercises and activities, plus a wealth of other reading-practice material, can be found at www.macmillanenglish.com/readers.

The Rich Brother

by Tobias Wolff

About the author

Tobias Wolff is a prolific[1] American author who is well known for his novels, short stories and memoirs, for which he has received a wide variety of awards. After serving in the US military and then working as a reporter for the *Washington Post*, Wolff went on to a long and distinguished academic career and is currently Professor of English and Creative Writing at Stanford University in California.

Born in 1945 in Birmingham, Alabama, Wolff's childhood was dramatic and disrupted. Wolff's early years were spent with his parents and older brother, Geoffrey. When his parents separated, the brothers were separated too: Geoffrey stayed with their father, and Tobias went with their mother to Florida. His mother's partner was violent and on two occasions she and Tobias had to run away for their safety, living first in Arizona, and then in Washington.

In Washington, his mother married again. Her new husband was obsessive and controlling and Wolff found his relationship with his new stepfather almost unbearable. This relationship and the claustrophobia[2] of his home life are described in Wolff's memoir, *This Boy's Life*, which was later made into a film by Martin Scorsese, starring Leonardo DiCaprio. This was not the only time that Wolff drew on his own experiences in his work.

When he was 16, Tobias was reunited with his older brother, Geoffrey, and the two became close. While Tobias had moved from school to school and achieved little academically, Geoffrey's schooling had been stable and successful.

When the two brothers were reunited, Geoffrey was at Princeton University. His academic success and commitment to writing were a big influence on Tobias, who – after a short time in the special forces

---

1 a prolific writer, band, etc produces a lot of books, CDs, etc
2 an uncomfortable feeling that you have when you think that you do not have enough freedom to do what you want

of the US Army, and service in Vietnam – went on to earn a First Class Honours degree at Oxford University in England, and a Masters degree at Stanford. Wolff's later adult life and career have been much more stable and conventional than his childhood. He is married and has three children. He taught at Syracuse University for 17 years before taking up his current position at Stanford in 1997.

Wolff has collaborated with other writers to edit short story collections, including *The Best American Short Stories* (1994). He has also continued to write and publish his own short story collections, including *In the Garden of the North American Martyrs* (1984), *Back in the World* (1985), *The Night in Question* (1996), and *Our Story Begins* (2008).

Wolff's first novel, *Ugly Rumours*, published in 1975, drew on his own experiences in the military, and tells the tale of two soldiers serving in Vietnam. He has since gone on to publish several other respected novellas[3] and novels, including, famously, *The Barracks Thief* (1984) and *Old School* (2003), which both received nominations for the PEN/Faulkner Award for Fiction[4] – *The Barracks Thief* winning the award in 1985.

Many of Wolff's stories focus on relationships, or a comparison between characters' perspectives, personalities and experiences. Known for the realism of his writing, the endings of Wolff's stories are often ambiguous, and the reader needs to make up their own mind about the characters and events in the stories.

About the story

The Rich Brother was first published in 1985 in the short story collection, *Back in the World*. The story uses a car journey to examine the characters of, and relationship between, two very different brothers, Pete and Donald.

3 short novels or stories, especially ones that teach a moral message
4 a national prize which honours the best published works of fiction by American citizens in a calendar year

Background information

Religious communities and alternative lifestyles

The story is set in the US state of California in the 1980s. The state is well known for its range of minority religious communities and churches. Since the 1960s it has been a place to which many have travelled to explore unusual spiritual beliefs and rituals. California provides many opportunities for people to explore lifestyles which are very different from those in conventional society, often living away from other towns and cities, isolated in 'closed communities', in small or large groups, following the teachings of a particular leader. This might mean wearing particular clothes, eating particular food or taking part in particular rituals and ceremonies. All of these things are done in the hope of finding God, peace, happiness, enlightenment or understanding.

Peru: Incas and gold

The Republic of Peru is a country in western South America. In the coastal regions in the west, the land is flat and dry and the climate is mild. The Andean highlands in the east reach up to 6,700 m at their highest peak. Further east of the mountains lies the Amazon rainforest, covering almost 60% of the country. The rainforest is mainly tropical, with heavy rainfall and high temperatures. Peru was home to the Inca Empire, a pre-Columbian[5] civilization which prized gold and silver very highly. These two precious metals were in abundant supply in Peru at the time, and continue to be important export products today, along with copper and zinc. Peru is one of the world's main gold producers and in 2010 hosted the Ninth International Gold Symposium.

5 referring to the period of history in the Americas before the Europeans arrived there

Summary

It may help you to know something about what happens in the story before you read it. Don't worry, this summary does *not* tell you how the story ends!

The Rich Brother is a story about two very different brothers. The older brother, Pete, leads a conventional and successful life – he works hard, is married with two children and is very wealthy. The younger brother, Donald, is single, rarely in work, and moves from place to place looking for spiritual fulfilment. Frequently, he has to ask Pete for money.

The story opens with Pete driving to pick up his brother from a farm outside Paso Robles, a town in California, where Donald has been living as part of a spiritual community.

On the journey, the two men talk about the community Donald has just left and about memories from their childhood. When the brothers stop for dinner, they meet a man called Webster, who claims to be on his way to visit his sick daughter. Without asking Pete, Donald offers Webster a ride. Webster joins the two brothers and entertains them with stories of his life and adventures. But his stories are received very differently by the two brothers and eventually lead to problems...

Pre-reading activities

Key vocabulary

This section will help you familiarize yourself with some of the more specific vocabulary used in the story. You may want to use it to help you before you start reading, or as a revision exercise after you have finished the story.

Cars

1 **The whole of the story takes place on a long car journey. Look at the short extracts below about the car (1–8) and match the words in bold with their definitions (a–i) below. (Note: For any American English words, the British English equivalent has been added in brackets.)**

1 *He looked at Pete, then stared out the **windshield** again.* (British: windscreen)

2 *Donald nodded. "I'll put my things in the **trunk**."* (British: boot)

3 *Donald balanced his drink on the **dashboard**, but the slight rocking of the car as he got out tipped it onto the **passenger's seat**.*

4 *Pete hit the **steering wheel** with the palm of his hand.*

5 *Pete took Donald's duffel bag from the backseat and set it down behind the car. He stood there, facing Donald in the red glow of the **taillights**.* (British: rear lights)

6 *Pete rummaged among his cassettes. He found Pachelbel's Canon and pushed it into the **tape deck**.*

7 *Pete looked into the **rearview mirror** and saw the man take another long puff before dropping the cigar out the window.*

8 *A line of trucks went past in the other direction, trailers festooned with **running lights**, engines roaring.*

a) a machine for playing music cassettes

b) the window at the front of the car

c) a place in the front of the car next to the driver

d) allows the driver to see what is happening behind the car while driving

e) the lights at the back of the car

f) lights that make a large vehicle more easily visible at night

g) allows the driver to control the direction of the car

h) the section inside the car which is in front of the driver and passenger

i) the section at the back of the car which is usually used for carrying luggage

Words relating to money

2 **One of the main themes of this story is wealth and money. Look at the words and their definitions on the next page and answer these questions.**

a) Which are verbs?
b) Which are related to the world of banks and finance?
c) Which two are particularly informal?
d) Which verb is related to being wealthy?
e) Which verb is related to not having any money?

---

broke not having any money

cash register a machine with containers for holding notes and coins that shows customers in shops how much they have to pay

interest money that you receive from an institution such as a bank when you keep money in an account there

prosper be successful, especially by making a lot of money

repossess take back something that someone had promised to pay you for over a period of time because they are unable to continue paying you for it

share one of the equal parts of a company that you can buy as a way of investing money

treat an occasion when you pay for something for someone else

trust fund an amount of money invested and managed for someone, often a child, by another person or organization

wad a thick roll or ball of banknotes

American English

3 **Look at the extracts below. Find the American English expression in each one and replace it with a British English expression from the box.**

---

the bill   car park   exhausted   motorway   open   our parents
a sailing boat   small coins   toilet

---

1 *He had two daughters, a sailboat, a house from which he could see a thin slice of the ocean, and friends doing well enough in their own lives not to wish bad luck on him.*

2 *Donald came up to the window. He bent down and said, "Thanks for coming. You must be totally whipped."*

3 *"I can't keep track of all these nickels and dimes," Pete said. "Just pay me back when your ship comes in."*

4 *Like when the folks went out at night and left you to babysit.*

5 *As Pete was paying the check he heard a man behind him say, "Excuse me, but I wonder if I might ask which direction you're going in?"*

6 *As soon as they left the parking lot the man lit a cigar.*

7 *"A cigar would make it easier."*
   Donald turned to Pete and said, "It's okay with me."
   "All right," Pete said. "Go ahead. Just keep the window rolled down."

8 *Donald pulled in at the next station they came to and filled the tank while Pete went to the men's room.*

9 *Afterward, on the highway, Donald said, "This is a new car, isn't it?"*

Colloquial and slang expressions

4 The author uses a lot of informal, colloquial expressions in the story. Look at the expressions in the box below and read the definitions. Do you have slang expressions in your own language for any of these things?

---

bug an insect
Caddy short for Cadillac, a type of car made in the US
cough up give someone some money
far out really strange
for keeps forever
get mad get angry
goofball *(mainly US)* a stupid person
hoot laugh
lingo language
nippy cold
phony fake, unreal
wised up understanding how things (and especially the world) work

---

Adjectives

5 Look at the following adjectives used to describe the two brothers, and their definitions. Which of the adjectives suggest:

1 a healthy lifestyle and a positive attitude?
2 a negative and possibly unhappy attitude?
3 an unhealthy lifestyle?

> **bony** so thin that the shape of the bones can be seen
> **gaunt** very thin, usually because you are ill, tired or worried
> **grave** very serious and worried
> **grim** very serious and unfriendly
> **hearty** friendly and enthusiastic
> **stout** *(polite)* slightly fat
> **upbeat** happy and optimistic
> **watchful** careful and possibly anxious

6 As you read the story, notice which of the adjectives in exercise 5 are used to describe which character.

Main themes

Before you read the story, you may want to think about some of its main themes. The questions will help you think about the story as you are reading it for the first time. There is more discussion of the main themes in the *Literary analysis* section after the story.

Brothers

The story describes the relationship, and especially the conflicts and differences, between two brothers. It explores themes of sibling rivalry (jealousy and competition between brothers and sisters) as well as of interdependence and family loyalty and responsibilities.

7 As you read the story, think about these questions:

a) In what ways are the brothers different?
b) Are they close? Do they worry about each other?
c) What does each brother want from the other?
d) What does each brother do for the other?
e) Do you think their relationship has changed by the end of the story?

Wealth and success

The story explores the question of what success is. Is it material, spiritual or both? It also explores the role money plays in bringing – or destroying – happiness, and its power to change and shape lives.

8 As you read the story, ask yourself:

a) How does each brother measure success?
b) Which brother do you think is more successful? Why?
c) Which brother do you think feels more successful?
d) What are the brothers' attitudes to each other's life choices?
e) What does Webster's story tell us about money, success and happiness?

Car journeys

Cars and long journeys by car are an important feature of the American way of life, and stories of car journeys are popular both in novels and in the cinema. During the car journey in *The Rich Brother*, three very different characters are forced to share a confined space for a considerable length of time. And it is the interaction between the characters, what they reveal and learn about themselves, that forms the focus of the story.

9 As you read the story, think about the following questions:

a) How is a conversation in a car different from a conversation elsewhere?
b) What responsibilities are involved in driving the car? Who takes care of each of these responsibilities?
c) In what way does the third passenger change the direction of the conversation when he joins the brothers in the car?

20

The Rich Brother

by Tobias Wolff

There were two brothers, Pete and Donald.

Pete, the older brother, was in **real estate**. He and his wife had a Century 21[6] **franchise** in Santa Cruz. Pete worked hard and made a lot of money, but not any more than he thought he deserved. He had two daughters, a sailboat, a house from which he could see a thin slice of the ocean, and friends doing well enough in their own lives not to wish bad luck on him. Donald, the younger brother, was still single. He lived alone, painted houses when he found the work, and got deeper in **debt** to Pete when he didn't.

No one would have taken them for brothers. Where Pete was stout and hearty and at home in the world, Donald was bony, grave, and obsessed with the fate of his soul. Over the years Donald had worn the images of two different Perfect Masters[7] around his neck. Out of devotion to the second of these he entered an ashram[8] in Berkeley, where he nearly died of **undiagnosed** hepatitis. By the time Pete finished paying the medical bills Donald had become a Christian. He drifted from church to church, then joined a Pentecostal[9] community that met somewhere in the Mission District[10] to sing **in tongues** and swap **prophecies**.

Pete couldn't make sense of it. Their parents were both dead, but while they were alive neither of them had found it necessary to believe that gods and devils were personally interested in

---

6 one of the world's largest estate agencies, with thousands of independently owned offices in the US and around the world

7 a person who has achieved spiritual enlightenment and guides others towards their understanding of God

8 the home of a small religious community of hindus

9 relating to a group of Christian churches that emphasize the power of the Holy Spirit

10 a neighbourhood in San Francisco

securing their company for all eternity. They managed to be decent people without making fools of themselves, and Pete had the same ambition. He thought the whole thing was an excuse for Donald to take himself seriously.

The trouble was that Donald couldn't content himself with worrying about his own soul. He had to worry about everyone else's, and especially Pete's. He handed down his judgments in ways he thought subtle: through significant silence, innuendo, looks of mild despair that said, *Brother, what have you come to?* What Pete had come to, as far as he could tell, was prosperity. That was the real issue between them. Pete prospered and Donald did not prosper.

———

At the age of forty Pete took up **skydiving**. He made his first jump with two friends who'd started only a few months earlier and were already doing **stunts**. Pete would never use the word "mystical", but that was how he felt about the experience. Later he made the mistake of describing it to Donald, who kept asking how much it cost and then acted **appalled** when Pete told him.

"At least I'm trying something new," Pete said. "At least I'm breaking the pattern."

Not long after that conversation Donald also broke the pattern, by moving to a farm outside Paso Robles. The farm was owned by several members of Donald's community, who'd bought it with the idea of forming a family of faith. That was how Donald explained it in the first letter he sent. Every week Pete heard how happy Donald was, how "in the Lord." He told Pete they were all praying for him, he and the rest of Pete's brothers and sisters on the farm.

I only have one brother, Pete wanted to answer, *and that's enough.* But he kept this thought to himself.

In November the letters stopped. Pete didn't worry about this at first, but when he called at Thanksgiving[11] Donald was grim. He tried to sound upbeat, but didn't try hard enough to make it

11 in the US and Canada, the day in November when families have a special meal, traditionally to celebrate all the things that they are grateful for

convincing. "Now listen," Pete said, "you don't have to stay in that place if you don't want to."

"I'll be all right," Donald answered.

"That's not the point. Being all right is not the point. If you don't like what's going on up there, then get out."

"I'm all right," Donald said again, more firmly. "I'm doing fine."

But he called Pete a week later and said that he was **quitting** the farm. When Pete asked him where he intended to go, Donald admitted that he had no plan. His car had been repossessed just before he left the city, and he was flat broke.

"I guess you'll have to stay with us," Pete said.

Donald put up a show of resistance. Then he gave in. "Just until I **get my feet on the ground**."

"Right," Pete said. "Check out your options." He told Donald he'd send him money for a bus ticket, but as they were about to **hang up** Pete changed his mind. He knew that Donald would try **hitchhiking** to save the fare, and he didn't want him out on the road all alone where some **creep** could pick him up, where anything could happen. "Better yet," he said, "I'll come and get you."

"You don't have to do that. I didn't expect you to do that," Donald said. "It's a pretty long drive."

"Just tell me how to get there."

But Donald wouldn't give him directions. He said the farm was too depressing, that Pete wouldn't like it. Instead, he insisted on meeting him at a **service station** called Jonathan's Mechanical Emporium.

"You must be kidding," Pete said.

"It's close to the highway," Donald told him. "I didn't name it."

"That's one for the collection," Pete said.

———

The day before he left to bring Donald home, Pete received a letter from a man who described himself as "head of household" at the farm where Donald had been living. He told Pete that Donald had not quit the farm but had been asked to leave. The letter was written on the back of a mimeographed[12] survey form asking people to record their response to a ceremony of some kind. The last question read:

What did you feel during the liturgy[13]?

a) Being

b) Becoming

c) Being and Becoming

d) None of the Above

e) All of the Above

Pete tried to forget the letter, but of course he couldn't. Each time he thought of it he felt crowded and breathless, the same feeling that came over him when he drove into the service station and saw his brother sitting against a wall with his head on his knees. It was late afternoon. A paper cup **tumbled** slowly past his feet, pushed by the damp wind.

Pete **honked** and Donald raised his head. He smiled at Pete, then stood and stretched. His arms were long and thin and white. He wore a red **bandanna** across his forehead and a T-shirt with a logo on the front that Pete couldn't read because the letters were inverted.

"Grow up," Pete yelled. "Get a Mercedes."

Donald came up to the window. He bent down and said, "Thanks for coming. You must be totally whipped."

"I'll make it." Pete pointed at the T-shirt. "What's that supposed to say?"

Donald looked down at his shirt front. "TRY GOD. I guess I put it on backwards. Pete, could I borrow a couple of dollars? I owe these people for coffee and sandwiches."

Pete took five twenties[14] from his wallet and held them out the window.

Donald stepped back as if horrified. "I don't need that much."

"I can't keep track of all these nickels and dimes[15]," Pete said.

---

12 *unusual, old-fashioned*: coming from a machine that makes copies of written, drawn or typed material
13 *religious*: a religious ceremony performed in church
14 *US, colloquial*: twenty-dollar banknotes.
15 *US, colloquial*: small coins that do not have much value – a 'nickel' is worth US5c; a 'dime' US10c

"Just pay me back **when your ship comes in**." He waved the bills impatiently. "Go on – take it."

"Only for now." Donald took the money and went into the service station. He came out carrying two orange sodas, one of which he handed to Pete as he got into the car. "My treat," he said.

"No bags?"

"Wow, thanks for reminding me." Donald balanced his drink on the dashboard, but the slight rocking of the car as he got out tipped it onto the passenger's seat, where half its contents **foamed over** before Pete could snatch it up again. Donald looked on while Pete held the bottle out the window, soda running down his fingers.

"Wipe it up," Pete told him. "Quick!"

"With what?"

Pete stared at him. "That shirt. Use the shirt."

Donald pulled a long face but did as he was told, his pale skin **puckering** against the wind.

"Great, just great," Pete said. "We haven't even left the gas[16] station yet."

Afterward, on the highway, Donald said, "This is a new car, isn't it?"

"Yes. This is a new car."

"Is that why you're so upset about the seat?"

"Forget it, okay? Let's just forget about it."

"I said I was sorry."

"I just wish you'd be more careful," Pete said. "These seats are made of leather. That stain won't come out, not to mention the smell. I don't see why I can't have leather seats that smell like leather instead of orange **pop**."

"What was wrong with the other car?"

Pete glanced over and saw that Donald had raised the **hood** of the blue sweatshirt he'd put on. The peaked hood above his gaunt, watchful face gave him the look of an **inquisitor**.

"There wasn't anything wrong with it," Pete said. "I just happened to like this one better."

16 US: petrol

Donald nodded.

There was a long silence between them as Pete drove on and the day darkened. On either side of the road lay **stubble**-covered fields. Low hills ran along the horizon, topped here and there with trees black against the evening sky. In the approaching line of cars a driver turned on his headlights. Pete did the same.

"So what happened?" he asked. "Farm life not your bag[17]?"

Donald took some time to answer, and at last he said, simply, "It was my fault."

"What was your fault?"

"The whole thing. Don't **play dumb**, Pete. I know they wrote to you." He looked at Pete, then stared out the windshield again.

"I'm not playing dumb."

Donald **shrugged**.

"All I really know is they asked you to leave," Pete went on. "I don't know any of the **particulars**."

"I blew it," Donald said. "Believe me, you don't want to hear **the gory details**."

"Sure I do," Pete said. He added, "Everybody likes the gory details."

"You mean everybody likes to hear how someone else messed up."

"Right," Pete said. "That's how it is here on Spaceship Earth."

Donald bent one knee onto the front seat and leaned against the door. Pete was aware of his **scrutiny**. He waited. Night was coming on in a rush, filling the **hollows** of the land. Donald's long cheeks and deep-set eyes were dark with shadow. His brow[18] was white. "Do you ever dream about me?" he asked.

"Do I ever dream about you? What kind of a question is that? Of course I don't dream about you," Pete said, untruthfully.

"What do you dream about?"

"Sex and money. Mostly money. A nightmare is when I dream I don't have any."

"You're just making that up," Donald said.

Pete smiled.

17 *slang, colloquial:* something that is not interesting to you personally
18 *literary:* forehead

"Sometimes I wake up at night," Donald went on "and I can tell you're dreaming about me."

"We were talking about the farm," Pete said. "Let's finish that conversation and then we can talk about our various out-of-body experiences and the interesting things we did during previous **incarnations**."

For a moment Donald looked like a **grinning skull**; then he turned serious again. "There's not that much to tell," he said. "I just didn't do anything right."

"That's a little vague," Pete said.

"Well, like the groceries. Whenever it was my turn to get the groceries I'd **blow** it somehow. I'd bring the groceries home and half of them would be missing, or I'd have all the wrong things, the wrong kind of flour or the wrong kind of chocolate or whatever. One time I gave them away. It's not funny, Pete."

Pete said, "Who'd you give the groceries to?"

"Just some people I picked up driving home. Some field-workers. They had about eight kids with them and didn't even speak English – just nodded their heads. Still, I shouldn't have given away the groceries. Not all of them, anyway. I really learned my lesson about that. You have to be practical. You have to be fair to yourself." Donald leaned forward, and Pete could sense his excitement. "There's nothing actually wrong with being in business," he said. "As long as you're fair to other people you can still be fair to yourself. I'm thinking of going into business, Pete."

"We'll talk about it," Pete said. "So, that's the story? There isn't any more to it than that?"

"What did they tell you?" Donald asked.

"Nothing."

"They must've told you something."

Pete shook his head.

"They didn't tell you about the fire?" When Pete shook his head again Donald regarded him for a time, then folded his arms across his chest and slumped back into the corner.

"Everybody had to take turns cooking dinner. I usually did

tuna **casserole** or spaghetti with garlic bread. But this one night I thought I'd do something different, something really interesting." He looked sharply at Pete. "It's all a big laugh to you, isn't it?"

"I'm sorry," Pete said.

"You don't know when to quit. You just keep hitting away."

"Tell me about the fire, Donald."

Donald kept watching him. "You have this **compulsion** to make me look foolish."

"Come off it, Donald. Don't make a big thing out of this."

"I know why you do it. It's because you don't have any purpose in life. You're afraid to relate to people who do, so you make fun of them."

"Relate," Pete said.

"You're basically a very frightened individual," Donald said. "Very threatened. You've always been like that. Do you remember when you used to try to kill me?"

"I don't have any compulsion to make you look foolish, Donald – you do it yourself. You're doing it right now."

"You can't tell me you don't remember," Donald said. "It was after my operation. You remember that."

"Sort of." Pete shrugged. "Not really."

"Oh yes," Donald said. "Do you want to see the scar?"

"I remember you had an operation. I don't remember the **specifics**, that's all. And I sure as hell don't remember trying to kill you."

"Oh yes," Donald repeated, maddeningly. "You bet your life you did. All the time. The thing was, I couldn't have anything happen to me where they sewed me up because then my **intestines** would come apart again and poison me. That was a big issue, Pete. Mom was always in a state about me climbing trees and so on. And you used to hit me there every chance you got."

"Mom was in a state every time you **burped**," Pete said. "I don't know. Maybe I bumped into you accidentally once or twice. I never did it deliberately."

"Every chance you got," Donald said. "Like when the folks went out at night and left you to babysit. I'd hear them say good night, and then I'd hear the car start up, and when they were gone I'd lie there and listen. After a while I could hear you coming down the hall, and I'd close my eyes and pretend to be asleep. There were nights when you'd stand outside the door, just stand there, and then go away again. But most nights you'd open the door and I'd hear you in the room with me, breathing. You'd come over and sit next to me on the bed – you remember, Pete, you have to – you'd sit next to me on the bed and pull the sheets back. If I was on my stomach you'd roll me over. Then you would lift up my pajama[19] top and start hitting me on my **stitches**. As hard as you could, over and over. I was afraid you'd get mad if you knew I was awake. Is that strange or what? I was afraid you'd get mad if you found out that I knew you were trying to kill me." Donald laughed. "Come on, you can't tell me you don't remember that."

"It might have happened once or twice. Kids do those things. I can't get all excited about something I maybe did twenty-five years ago."

"No maybe about it. You did it."

Pete said, "You're wearing me out with this stuff. We've got a long drive ahead of us, and if you don't back off pretty soon we aren't going to make it. You aren't, anyway."

Donald turned away.

"I'm doing my best," Pete said. The self-pity in his voice made this sound like a lie. But it wasn't a lie. He *was* doing his best.

The car topped a rise[20]. In the distance Pete saw a **cluster** of lights that **blinked** out when he started downhill. There was no moon. The sky was low and black.

"Come to think of it," Pete said, "I did have a dream about you the other night. Quite a few nights ago, actually. Are you hungry?"

"What kind of dream?"

"It was strange. You were taking care of me. Just the two of us.

19 *US spelling:* pyjamas – clothes that you wear in bed
20 *literary:* reached the top of a hill

I don't know where everyone else was supposed to be."

Pete left it at that. He didn't tell Donald that in this dream he was blind.

"I wonder if that was when I woke up," Donald said. "Look, I'm sorry I got into that thing about my scar. I keep trying to forget it but I guess I never will. Not really. It was pretty strange, having someone around all the time who wanted to get rid of me."

"Kid stuff," Pete said. "Ancient history."

———

They ate dinner at a Denny's[21] on the other side of King City. As Pete was paying the check he heard a man behind him say, "Excuse me, but I wonder if I might ask which direction you're going in?"

Donald answered, "Santa Cruz."

"Perfect," the man said.

Pete could see him in the fish-eye mirror above the cash register: a red **blazer** with some kind of **crest** on the pocket, little black mustache[22], glossy black hair combed down on his forehead like a Roman emperor's. A *rug*[23] Peter thought. *Definitely a rug.*

He got his change and turned. "Why is that perfect?" he asked.

The man looked at Pete. He had a soft **ruddy** face that was doing its best to express pleasant surprise, as if this new **wrinkle** were all he could have wished for, but the eyes behind the aviator glasses[24] showed signs of regret. His lips were moist and shiny. "I take it you're together," he said.

"You got it," Pete told him.

"All the better, then," the man went on. "It so happens I'm going to Santa Cruz myself. Had a spot of car trouble down the road. The old Caddy let me down."

"What kind of trouble?" Pete asked.

"Engine trouble," the man said. "I'm afraid it's a bit urgent.

21 a chain of fast-food and steakhouse restaurants in the US
22 *US spelling:* moustache
23 *colloquial:* a wig, or hairpiece to cover a bald patch on the head
24 a style of sunglasses typically worn by aircraft pilots

My daughter is sick. Urgently sick. I've got a **telegram** here." He patted the breast pocket of his blazer.

Before Pete could say anything Donald got into the act again. "No problem," he said. "We've got **tons** of room."

"Not that much room," Pete said.

Donald nodded. "I'll put my things in the trunk."

"The trunk's full," Pete told him.

"It so happens I'm traveling[25] light," the man said. "This **leg** of the trip, anyway. In fact I don't have any luggage at this particular time."

Pete said, "Left it in the old Caddy, did you?"

"Exactly," the man said.

"No problem," Donald repeated. He walked outside, and the man went with him, Pete following at a distance. When they reached Pete's car Donald raised his face to the sky, and the man did the same. They stood there looking up. "Dark night," Donald said.

"Stygian[26]," the man said.

Pete still had it in mind to **brush him off**, but he didn't. Instead he unlocked the car and opened the back door for him. He wanted to see what would happen. It was an adventure, though not a dangerous adventure. The man might steal Pete's ashtrays but he wouldn't kill him. If anyone killed Pete on the road it would be some spiritual person in a sweat suit[27], someone with his eyes on the far horizon and a wet TRY GOD T-shirt in his **duffel bag**.

As soon as they left the parking lot the man lit a cigar. He blew a cloud of smoke over Pete's shoulder and sighed with pleasure.

"Put it out," Pete told him.

"Of course," the man said. Pete looked into the rearview mirror and saw the man take another long **puff** before dropping the cigar out the window. "Forgive me," he said. "I should have asked. Name's Webster, by the way."

25 *US spelling:* travelling
26 *mainly literary:* dark and frightening; the river Styx in Greek mythology forms the boundary between Earth and the Underworld
27 *US:* a jogging suit

Donald turned and looked back at him. "First name or last?"

The man hesitated. "Last," he said finally.

"I know a Webster," Donald said. "Mick Webster."

"There are many of us," Webster said.

"Big fellow, wooden leg," Pete said.

Donald gave Pete a look.

Webster shook his head. "Doesn't **ring a bell**. Still, I wouldn't deny the connection. Might be one of the cousinry[28]."

"What's your daughter got?" Pete asked.

"That isn't clear," Webster answered. "It appears to be a female complaint of some nature. Then again it may be tropical." He was quiet for a moment, and added: "If indeed it *is* tropical, I will have to assume some of the blame myself. It was my own vaulting ambition[29] that first led us to the tropics[30] and kept us there all those many years, **exposed** to every evil. Truly, I have much to answer for. I left my wife there."

"You mean she died?" Donald asked.

"I buried her with these hands. The earth will be repaid, gold for gold."

"Which tropics?" Pete asked.

"The tropics of Peru."

"What part of Peru are they in?"

"The lowlands," Webster said.

"What's it like down there? In the lowlands."

"Another world," Webster said. His tone was sepulchral[31]. "A world better imagined than described."

"Far out," Pete said.

The three men rode in silence for a time. A line of trucks went past in the other direction, trailers festooned[32] with running lights, engines roaring.

---

28 *unusual:* a collection of cousins

29 *literary:* from Shakespeare's play *Macbeth* – refers to a desire to succeed at something that is more important to someone than anything else in their life

30 the hottest part of the Earth, between the Tropic of Cancer and the Tropic of Capricorn

31 *literary, religious, unusual:* relating to death or a tomb; dark and frightening

32 *unusual:* decorated

"Yes," Webster said at last, "I have much to answer for."

Pete smiled at Donald, but he'd turned in his seat again and was gazing at Webster. "I'm sorry about your wife," Donald said.

"What did she die of?" Pete asked.

"A **wasting** illness," Webster said. "The doctors have no name for it, but I do." He leaned forward and said, fiercely, "*Greed.* Mine, not hers. She wanted no part of it."

Pete bit his lip. Webster was a **find**, and Pete didn't want to scare him off by hooting at him. In a voice low and innocent of knowingness, he asked, "What took you there?"

"It's difficult for me to talk about."

"Try," Pete told him.

"A cigar would make it easier."

Donald turned to Pete and said, "It's okay with me."

"All right," Pete said. "Go ahead. Just keep the window rolled down."

"Much obliged[33]." A match flared. There were eager sucking sounds.

"Let's hear it," Pete said.

"I am by training an engineer," Webster began. "My work has exposed me to all but one of the continents, to desert and alp and forest, to every terrain and season of the earth. Some years ago I was hired by the Peruvian government to search for tungsten[34] in the tropics. My wife and daughter accompanied me. We were the only white people for a thousand miles in any direction, and we had no choice but to live as the Indians lived – to share their food and drink and even their culture."

"You knew the lingo, did you?" Pete said.

"We picked it up." The **ember** of the cigar bobbed up and down. "We were used to learning as necessity decreed[35]. At any rate, it became evident after a couple of years that there was no tungsten to be found. My wife had fallen ill and was pleading to be taken home. But I was deaf to her pleas, because by then

33 *old-fashioned:* 'thank you'; 'I'm very grateful'
34 a very hard metal used for making steel
35 *formal, legal:* if a leader or government decrees something, they officially decide or order it

I was on the trail of another metal – a metal far more valuable than tungsten."

"Let me guess," Pete said. "Gold?"

Donald looked at Pete, then back at Webster.

"Gold," Webster said. "A vein of gold greater than the Mother Lode[36] itself. After I found the first traces of it nothing could tear me away from my search – not the sickness of my wife nor anything else. I was determined to uncover the vein, and so I did, but not before I **laid my wife to rest**. As I say, the earth will be repaid."

Webster was quiet. Then he said, "But life must go on. In the years since my wife's death I've been making the necessary arrangements to open the mine. I could have done it immediately, of course, enriching myself beyond measure[37], but I knew what that would mean – the exploitation of our beloved Indians, the **brutal** destruction of their environment. I felt I had too much to atone for already." Webster paused, and when he spoke again his voice was dull and rushed, as if he'd used up all the interest he had in his own words. "Instead I drew up a program for returning **the bulk of** the wealth to the Indians themselves. A kind of trust fund. The interest alone will allow them to secure their ancient lands and rights in perpetuity[38]. At the same time, our investors will be rewarded a thousandfold[39]. Two thousandfold. Everyone will prosper together."

"That's great," Donald said. "That's the way it ought to be."

Pete said, "I'm willing to bet you have a few shares left. Am I right?"

Webster made no reply.

"Well?" Pete knew that Webster was on to him now, but he didn't care. The story had bored him. He'd expected something different, something original, and Webster had let him down. He hadn't even tried. Pete felt **sour** and **stale**. His eyes burned from cigar smoke and the high beams of road-hogging truckers.

36 *mainly US:* a very large amount of silver, gold, coal, etc under the ground
37 *mainly literary:* in such large quantities that they cannot be measured
38 *legal:* for all time in the future
39 *formal:* a thousand times as much. The suffix *-fold* is used with numbers to make adjectives and adverbs describing how much something increases

"Douse the stogie[40]," he said to Webster. "I told you to keep the window down."

"Got a little nippy back here."

"Hey, Pete," Donald said. "Lighten up."

"Douse it!"

Webster sighed, then slipped the cigar out the window.

"I'm a **wreck**," Pete said to Donald. "You want to drive for a while?"

"Too much[41]! I was just about to offer! I mean, the words were right on the tip of my tongue."

Pete pulled over and they changed places.

Webster **kept his own counsel** in the backseat. Donald hummed while he drove, until Pete told him to stop. Then everything went quiet.

Donald was humming again when Pete woke up. He stared sullenly at the road, at the white lines sliding past the car. After a few moments of this he turned and said, "How long have I been out?"

Donald glanced at him. "Twenty, twenty-five minutes."

Pete looked behind him and saw that Webster was gone. "Where's our friend?"

"You just missed him. He got out in Soledad. He told me to say thanks and good-bye."

"Soledad? What about his sick daughter? How did he explain her away?"

"He has a brother living there. He's going to borrow a car from him and drive the rest of the way in the morning."

"I'll bet his brother's living there," Pete said. "Doing fifty **concurrent life sentences**. His brother and his sister and his mom and his dad."

"I kind of liked him," Donald said.

"I'm sure you did," Pete said.

"He was interesting. He'd been places."

"His cigars had been places, I'll give you that."

"Come on, Pete."

40 *slang:* extinguish/put out the cigar
41 *mainly US, informal:* a phrase used to express surprise or amusement

"Come on yourself. What a phony."

"You don't know that."

"Sure I do."

"How? How do you know?"

Pete stretched. "Brother, there are some things you're just born knowing. What's the gas situation?"

"We're a little low."

"Then why didn't you get some more?"

"I wish you wouldn't snap at me like that," Donald said.

"Then why don't you use your head? What if we run out?"

"We'll make it," Donald said. "I'm pretty sure we've got enough to make it. You didn't have to be so rude to him."

"I don't feel like running out of gas tonight, okay?"

Donald pulled in at the next station they came to and filled the tank while Pete went to the men's room. When Pete came back, Donald was sitting in the passenger's seat. As Pete got in behind the wheel the attendant came up to his window, bent down, and said, "Twenty-one fifty-five."

"You heard the man," Pete said to Donald.

Donald looked straight ahead. He didn't move.

"Cough up," Pete said. "This trip's on you."

"I can't."

"Sure you can. Break out that wad."

"Please," he said. "Pete, I don't have it anymore."

Pete took this in. He nodded, and paid the attendant.

Donald began to speak when they pulled out but Pete cut him off. He said, "I don't want to hear from you right now. You just keep quiet or I swear to God I won't be responsible."

They left the fields and entered a forest of tall pines. The trees went on and on. "Let me get this straight," Pete said at last. "You don't have the money I gave you."

"You treated him like a bug or something," Donald said.

"You don't have the money," Pete said again.

Donald shook his head.

"Since I bought dinner, and since we didn't stop anywhere in between, I assume you gave it to Webster. Is that right? Is that what you did with it?"

"Yes."

Pete looked at Donald. His face was dark under the hood but he still managed to convey a sense of remove[42], as if none of this had anything to do with him.

"Why?" Pete asked. "Why did you give it to him?" When Donald didn't answer, Pete said, "A hundred dollars, gone. Just like that. I *worked* for that money, Donald."

"I know, I know," Donald said.

"You don't know! How could you? You get money by holding out your hand."

"I work too," Donald said.

"You work too? Don't **kid yourself**, brother." Donald leaned toward him, about to say something, but Pete cut him off again. "You're not the only person on the payroll,[43] Donald. I don't think you understand that. I have a family."

"Pete, I'll pay you back."

"Like hell you will. A hundred dollars!" Pete hit the steering wheel with the palm of his hand. "Just because you think I hurt some goofball's feelings. Jesus, Donald."

"That's not the reason," Donald said. "And I didn't just *give* him the money."

"What do you call it, then? What do you call what you did?"

"I *invested* it. I wanted a share, Pete." When Pete looked over at him Donald nodded and said again, "I wanted a share."

Pete said, "I take it you're referring to the gold mine in Peru."

"Yes," Donald said.

"You believe that such a gold mine exists?"

Donald looked at him, and Pete could see he was just beginning to **catch on**. "You'll believe anything, won't you?" Pete said. "You really will believe anything at all."

"I'm sorry," Donald said, and turned away.

---

42 *literary*: a feeling of detachment
43 *poetic use*: literally, employed by a particular company – here used to refer to Pete's family, for which he has financial responsibility

Pete drove on between the trees and considered the truth of what he'd just said – that Donald would believe anything at all. And it came to him that it would be just like this unfair life for Donald to come out ahead in the end, by believing in some outrageous promise that turned out to be true and that he, Pete, rejected out of hand because he was too wised up to listen to anybody's **pitch** anymore, except for laughs. What a joke. What a joke if there really was a **blessing** to be had, and the blessing didn't come to the one who deserved it, the one who did all the work, but to the other.

And as if this had already happened Pete felt a shadow move upon him, darkening his thoughts. After a time he said, "I can see where all this is going, Donald."

"I'll pay you back," Donald said.

"No," Pete said. "You won't pay me back. You can't. You don't know how. All you've ever done is take. All your life."

Donald shook his head.

"I see exactly where this is going," Pete went on. "You can't work, you can't take care of yourself, you believe anything anyone tells you. I'm stuck with you, aren't I?" He looked over at Donald. "I've got you on my hands **for good**."

Donald pressed his fingers against the dashboard as if to brace himself. "I'll get out," he said.

Pete kept driving.

"Let me out," Donald said. "I mean it, Pete."

"Do you?"

Donald hesitated. "Yes," he said.

"Be sure," Pete told him. "This is it. This is for keeps."

"I mean it."

"All right. You made the choice." Pete braked the car sharply and swung onto the shoulder. He turned off the engine and got out. Trees **loomed** on both sides of the road, shutting out the sky. The air was cold and **musty**. Pete took Donald's duffel bag from the backseat and set it down behind the car. He stood there, facing Donald in the red glow of the taillights. "It's better this way," Pete said.

Donald just looked at him.

"Better for you," Pete said.

Donald hugged himself. He was shaking. "You don't have to say all that," he told Pete. "I don't blame you."

"Blame me? What the hell are you talking about? Blame me for what?"

"For anything," Donald said.

"I want to know what you mean about blaming me."

"Nothing. Nothing, Pete. You'd better get going. God bless you."

"That's it," Pete said, and took a step toward Donald.

Donald touched Pete's shoulder. "You'd better go," he said.

Somewhere in the trees overhead a branch snapped. Pete looked up, and felt the **fists** he'd made of his hands. He turned his back on Donald and walked to the car and drove away. He drove fast, **hunched** over the wheel, conscious of how he was hunched and the **shallowness** of his breathing, refusing to look at the mirror above his head until there was nothing behind him but darkness.

Then he said, "A hundred dollars," as if there was someone to hear.

The trees gave way to fields. Pete drove on between metal fences **plastered** with windblown scraps of paper. Tule[44] fog hung above the **ditches**, spilling into the road, dimming the ghostly halogen lights that burned in the yards of the farms he passed. The fog left **beads** of water rolling up the windshield.

Pete **rummaged** among his cassettes. He found Pachelbel's Canon[45] and pushed it into the tape deck. When the violins began to play he leaned back and assumed an attentive expression, as if he really were listening to them. He smiled to himself like a man at liberty to enjoy music, a man who has finished work and settled his debts, done all things meet[46] and **due**.

44 *unusual, literary:* coming from swampy land
45 a famous piece of music by German Baroque composer Johann Pachelbel (1653– 1706)
46 *old-fashioned:* right or suitable

And in this way, smiling, nodding to the music, he went another mile or two and pretended that he was not already slowing down, that he wouldn't turn back, that he would be able to drive on like this, alone, and have the right answer when his wife stood before him in the doorway of his home and asked, *Where is he? Where is your brother?*

Post-reading activities

Understanding the story

Use these questions to help you check that you have understood the story.

Introduction

1 What is Pete's job?
2 What kind of lifestyle has he got?
3 What does Donald do?
4 Why doesn't Pete understand Donald's way of life?
5 Why did Pete start skydiving? What was Donald's reaction?

Paso Robles

6 Why did Donald move to the farm in Paso Robles?
7 Did he like it there?
8 When did things change? How do we know?
9 Why did Donald phone Pete?
10 What did Pete offer to do? Why?
11 Where did they arrange to meet? Why?

The first leg of the journey

12 How does Pete feel about the letter from the farm? Why does he feel this way?
13 Why does Donald ask Pete for money?
14 How much money does Pete give him?
15 Why is Pete so upset about the spilled drink?
16 Why does Donald ask Pete about his old car?
17 Who starts the conversation about the farm?
18 Is Donald happy to talk about it?
19 Why does Donald ask Pete whether he dreams about him?
20 Why does Pete lie to him about his dreams?
21 What did Donald do with the groceries? Why? What lesson did it teach him?
22 Why does Donald get angry with Pete when he is talking about the fire at the farm?
23 What does Donald accuse Pete of doing to him when he was a child?
24 What is Pete's reaction to the accusation?
25 Why does Pete tell Donald about his dream? Why doesn't he tell him all the details?

26 Why do the brothers stop the car?
27 Who do they meet? What does this person want?
28 What is Pete's first impression of Webster?
29 Is Pete happy about giving Webster a lift?
30 How does each brother feel about Webster and his stories?
31 What does Webster say he trained as originally? What took him to Peru?
32 Why does Webster say that he did not open the gold mine when his wife died, when he was still in Peru?
33 What does Webster say he did for the native Peruvian Indian population?
34 Does Pete believe Webster's stories? Do you believe them? Why/ Why not?
35 What does Pete ask Donald when he wakes up?
36 What reason does Donald give Pete for Webster getting out at Soledad?
37 Why does Pete get angry with Donald?
38 Why does Donald ask to get out of the car?
39 What is Pete doing at the end of the story?

Language study

Using *would* to talk about the past

In the story, Donald challenges Pete about the violence he inflicted on him when they were children. He often uses the modal verb *would* to talk about these past events.

1 Look at this passage from the story. Underline all the examples of *would*.

I'd hear them say good night, and then I'd hear the car start up, and when they were gone I'd lie there and listen. After a while I could hear you coming down the hall, and I'd close my eyes and pretend to be asleep. There were nights when you'd stand outside the door, just stand there, and then go away again. But most nights you'd open the door and I'd hear you in the room with me, breathing. You'd come over and sit next to me on the bed – you remember, Pete, you have to – you'd sit next to me on the bed and pull the sheets back. If I was on my stomach you'd roll me over. Then you would lift up my pajama top and start hitting me on my stitches.

2 **Look again at the words you have underlined in the passage in exercise 1. Which one of the following describes the use of *would* in the passage?**

a) single actions that happened once at a specific time in the past
b) actions that were repeated regularly in the past

Used to and *would*

We use both *used to* and *would* to talk about past habits and repeated actions:

> *I'd pretend to be asleep. / I used to pretend to be asleep.*

We only use *would* to describe actions – we have to use *used to* to describe states:

> ~~I'd be~~ **I used to be** *afraid of you.*

3 **Look at the sentences below. When can you substitute *used to* with *would*?**

1 The two brothers used to be very good friends.
2 Pete used to look after his little brother when his parents went out.
3 Donald used to be in bed when his parents left the house.
4 He used to think his brother wanted to kill him.
5 Pete sometimes used to listen outside his door.
6 At other times he used to go into the room and wake Donald up.

4 **Look again at the sentences in exercise 3. Which are true and which are false, according to what the story tells us?**

Notice how *would* can be dropped when there is a list of verbs with the same subject:

> *I'd close my eyes and (I'd) pretend to be asleep.*

5 **Delete all the unnecessary examples of *would* in the following text.**

There were nights when you'd stand outside the door, you'd just stand there, and then you'd go away again. But most nights you'd open the door and I'd hear you in the room with me, breathing. You'd come over and you'd sit next to me on the bed – you remember, Pete, you have to – you'd sit next to me on the bed and you'd pull the sheets back.

Compare your answers with the original extract in exercise 1.

Phrasal verbs

Phrasal verbs are multi-word verbs that consist of a verb plus one or two particles. These particles can be prepositions or adverbs. The author uses a lot of phrasal verbs in the story, both in the narrative and in the dialogue.

6 Find 11 phrasal verbs in the extracts below.

1 *At the age of forty Pete took up skydiving.*
2 *If you don't like what's going on up there, then get out.*
3 *He didn't want him out on the road all alone where some creep could pick him up, where anything could happen.*
4 *"Grow up," Pete yelled. "Get a Mercedes."*
5 *Just pay me back when your ship comes in.*
6 *In the approaching line of cars a driver turned on his headlights.*
7 *I'd bring the groceries home and half of them would be missing…One time I gave them away.*
8 *You're wearing me out with this stuff.*
9 *I'm sorry I got into that thing about my scar.*

The meaning of some phrasal verbs can be understood from the meaning of the various parts, eg *come in* (move + from outside to inside) = enter. But this is not true of all phrasal verbs, eg *give up* = to stop doing something.

7 Match the phrasal verbs in exercise 6 with their equivalents in the box.

arrives	be mature	give me the money	give him a lift
happening	leave	started	making me tired	switched on
let someone have them for free	began to discuss		

8 Look at the following description of phrasal verb types and then find one example of each in the sentences in exercise 6.

There are three basic types of two-word phrasal verbs:

Type 1: intransitive – it has no object: *sit down, drink up,* ....

Type 2: transitive, inseparable – the object always follows the particle: *He got on the bus,* ....

Type 3: transitive, separable – the object can come between the verb and the particle (and when it is a pronoun it *must* come between the verb and the particle): *Pete took up skydiving (he took it up last year),*

....

<u>Tip:</u> If you want to know if a phrasal verb is separable or inseparable, try saying it with an object pronoun (*me, you, him, her*, etc). Alternatively, look it up in a good dictionary – the examples will show you whether or not the object pronoun should come before or after the particle.

9 Write the words in italics in the correct order to make phrasal verbs.

1 *The old Caddy* **me down let**.
2 *Pete still had it in mind to* **off him brush**.
3 *"* **it out put**,*" Pete told him*.
4 *Pete didn't want to* **him off scare**.
5 *Life* **go must on**.
6 *You just missed him.* **out got he** *in Soledad*.
7 *Donald began to speak when* **pulled they out**…
8 *…but Pete* **cut off him**.

Literary analysis

Plot

1 What are the key events in the story? Which event/s happened before the journey in the car?
2 What time of day does the car journey take place? How long does the main action in the story last?
3 At times during the story, Pete and Donald chat quite easily and even tease each other. However, they also have lots of squabbles (small arguments). Look back at the story – what comment or sensitivity is the cause of each squabble?
4 What do you think happens after the story finishes?

Character

5 What do we know about the two main characters? They are very different in a lot of ways, but do they have anything in common?
6 Think back to the eight adjectives that you looked at in Pre-reading exercise 5. Which adjectives describe which character? What do the adjectives tell us about their personalities?
7 What other adjectives would you use to describe the character of each brother?
8 What adjectives would the brothers use, do you think, to describe each other?

9   What does Pete's dream tell you about his feelings towards his
     brother? Why do you think Pete does not tell Donald that he was
     blind in the dream? What do you think the dream means?
10   What does the encounter with Webster tell us about each brother?
11   The author gives us a very clear description of Webster. Why
     do you think he does this? What do you think this description
     suggests about Webster's character? Why?
12   Why does Donald give Webster his money? What does Donald's
     attitude to Webster's stories about gold tell us about Donald?
13   Looking at the story as a whole, which of the two brothers do you
     think is 'The Rich Brother'? Why?

Narration

14   Who tells the story? From which character's point of view? How
     would the story have been different if it had been told from the
     point of view of the other characters? What information would
     have been added or lost?
15   Almost all of the action in the story takes place in the car. What
     changes take place in the world outside the car? What effect does
     this have on the story? What effect does this have on how the
     relationship between the brothers is described? How does it affect
     their conversation?
16   Why do you think the author introduces Webster into the story?
     How does Webster's presence, and then departure, affect the
     atmosphere in the car?
17   How does the author make it clear that Pete will go back to get
     Donald at the end of the story?

Style

18   Look at the opening sentence and how it introduces the story:

     There were two brothers, Pete and Donald.

     What is the effect of this simple, one-sentence paragraph? How
     is the opening sentence mirrored in the three paragraphs which
     follow it?
19   Notice how the last sentence of the fifth paragraph echoes the
     structure of the opening sentence:

     Pete prospered and Donald did not prosper.

     Is the relationship between the two brothers really that simple?

20 A lot of the story is told through dialogue. What effect does this create? In what ways do you think direct speech can be more effective than reported speech?

21 Look at the first conversation between the brothers as they meet in the gas station and then take to the road. How does the dialogue reflect the change in the mood?

22 Look again at how Webster tells his story. Notice how he often uses formal or archaic[47] language. What effect does this create?

23 The dialogue is sometimes interrupted by brief descriptions of the landscape outside the car. Each description is followed by a new attempt at conversation. Look at one of these descriptions below. What atmosphere does it convey? How does it calm the brothers' nerves?

The car topped a rise. In the distance Pete saw a cluster of lights that blinked out when he started downhill. There was no moon. The sky was low and black.

24 Look at the following description, which is given after Donald asks Pete to let him out of the car. In what way is the atmosphere different? How has this new atmosphere been created? Underline the specific words in the description that add to the atmosphere.

Pete braked the car sharply and swung onto the shoulder. He turned off the engine and got out. Trees loomed on both sides of the road, shutting out the sky. The air was cold and musty.

25 Read the last paragraph again. Notice the contrast between what is said and what we know is going to happen. Why will Pete finally turn round and go back for his brother?

Guidance to the above literary terms, answer keys to all the exercises and activities, plus a wealth of other reading-practice material, can be found at www.macmillanenglish.com/readers.

47 old and no longer used

The Blood Bay

by Annie Proulx

About the author

Edna Annie Proulx was born in Connecticut in 1935, the eldest of five girls. Her French Canadian father worked in textiles and because of his job the family moved frequently within the US, the young Proulx living in various places in New England and North Carolina. Proulx's mother was a painter, who encouraged her children in what she called 'the art of observation'. Proulx credits her grandmother with teaching her 'the facility of shaping a story'.

As a child, Proulx dreamed of becoming a concert violinist. Despite her discipline and commitment, this was not to be, and after finishing high school Proulx instead attended Colby College for a short time. Impulsively, she left to marry her first husband with whom she had a daughter.

When the marriage ended, and her ex-husband took custody[1] of her daughter, Proulx briefly married again. After her second divorce, she went to the University of Vermont to study for her bachelor's degree. In 1969 she graduated, and married for a third time – she and James Hamilton Lang lived together with Proulx's two sons from her second marriage, as well as having a son of their own.

Proulx then returned to study and earned her master's degree at Sir George Williams University[2] in Montreal, Canada. After that, she began to study for a doctorate.

When her third marriage also ended Proulx decided she was not suited to a traditional family unit. She abandoned her doctorate and settled in Vermont, where she began writing to support her three sons.

---

1 *legal*: the right to look after a child
2 now called Concordia University

Proulx's freelance[3] career led her to write on a wide range of different subjects from African beadwork to fishing. She loved the rural life and enjoyed fishing, hunting, canoeing, skiing and exploring and interacting with her surroundings. She became involved in the 'back-to-the-land movement'[4], and among other things, published her own cookbook, and a guide to *The Fine Art of Salad Gardening* (1985). Proulx also created her own newspaper, *Behind the Times*, which ran for two years, and began to write short stories. In 1988, she published her first short story collection, *Heart Songs and Other Stories*. Her first novel, *Postcards*, was published in 1992 and earned her the PEN/Faulkner Award for Fiction. *The Shipping News* followed and received many awards, including the 1994 Pulitzer Prize[5] for Fiction. It was later made into a film.

When her youngest son moved away from home, leaving her alone for the first time in her life, Proulx felt a freedom she had not experienced before, and celebrated this by travelling across the States in her truck every year. Describing herself as 'deeply moved' by the vast landscape, she settled in Wyoming, and in 1999 released *Close Range: Wyoming Stories*. This collection included the short story *Brokeback Mountain*, the film version of which was nominated for eight Oscars in 2006.

Success has brought many benefits, including the time to write more, and to work with an architect to design and build her own house by huge cliffs on the shores of the North Platte River, Wyoming, the main purpose of which is to house her huge collection of books. Although she is known for being a great hostess, has many valued friends and is now reunited with her daughter, the solitude of her chosen home suits the author for whom landscape is such a key feature of her writing.

---

3   selling your services to more than one company rather than being permanently employed by a particular one
4   a social phenomenon in North America in the 1960s and 1970s where people left the cities to live in the country
5   highly prestigious American awards given annually for achievements in journalism, literature and musical composition

About the story

The Blood Bay was first published in 1999 in Proulx's short story collection *Close Range: Wyoming Stories*.

Background information

Cowboys

A cowboy's main job is to take care of cattle (cows for beef, also called steers) traditionally on horseback. They also have a variety of other duties around the land, working for a ranch – a large farm. Cowboys can be seen across North, Central and South America. The role of cowboys in the United States is critical to the American identity. Famous Hollywood actors such as John Wayne have depicted cowboys as strong, brave men in iconic films about the hardship of life in the American Midwest[6]. They were seen as the adventurers of the American Wild West[7].

As the geography, climate and infrastructure of cattle handling and land management has changed, the cowboy's role has also had to adapt, but many traditions still remain. Cowboys still lead difficult and dangerous lives – riding long distances on horseback, catching cattle and braving wolves, snakes and other dangerous animals, as well as travelling, eating and sleeping in extreme temperatures. They carry guns to protect themselves from animals and other men.

The cowboys in the story are cowpunchers, cowboys who find and count cattle. They round up[8] cattle in the snow, find strays – steers that have been separated from the rest of the cattle – and bring them back to the herd, and rescue cattle that have got bogged down (stuck up to their necks or stomachs) in the deep snow.

6   the states in the central region of the US
7   the western part of the US during the period of time when towns and cities developed. There was a lot of violence, especially between the new people arriving and the native Americans who lived there already
8   bring animals or people together in one place for a particular purpose

Wyoming

Wyoming is the 10th largest state in the US by geographical area but the smallest in terms of population, with just over half a million inhabitants. That equates to an average of just under two people per square kilometre. The land is hard and dry, in the west are the Rocky Mountains, and in the east the High Plains – a high elevation of prairie (a large, flat area of grassland) suited mainly to rearing cattle. In the summer it can be very hot during the day, with temperatures rising to 35°C or higher. The winters are very cold. The mountain areas get up to five metres or more of snow a year, with frequent strong winds and blizzards (snowstorms). Agriculture has always been an important component of Wyoming's economy and is still an essential part of the state's culture and lifestyle. More than 91% of Wyoming is classified as rural.

The story takes place on the banks of the Powder River, which flows from Montana into Wyoming, covering more than 600 kilometres before it runs into the Yellowstone River. The Powder River Basin is traditional cattle-driving territory. The cowboy who is described at the beginning of the story has ridden south from Montana and is found by an outfit (a group of cowboys working together) who take their name from Box Spring, a geyser (hot water spring) in Yellowstone National Park, Wyoming.

Blood bay

Blood bay is a term used to describe a type of horse whose coat is a rich reddish brown with a black mane, tail, ear edges and lower legs. This colouring is common in many breeds of horses, including those used by cowboys, and there are many different types of bay with coats of various different shades of brown. Horses are often referred to by the colour of their coat, for example a grey, a palomino or a bay. However, this is not the case for all horse colours – for example you cannot say 'a white' or 'a black'.

Summary

It may help you to know something about what happens in the story before you read it. Don't worry, this summary does *not* tell you how the story ends!

During a freezing night on the plains of Wyoming, a young cowboy freezes to death because he does not have enough warm clothes, having spent his money on some handmade leather boots instead. The next day, three more experienced and properly dressed cowboys pass his dead body; one of them, 'Dirt Sheets', notices he has the same size feet as the dead man and decides to take the boots, as his own are not in good condition. The boots are frozen onto the dead body, so he cuts off both feet with the boots still on, and decides to thaw[9] them by the fire that evening and take off the boots then.

That night, the cowboys stay at old man Grice's house. The old man warns them to be careful of one of his horses, a blood bay, saying it bites. The cowboys share a meal and play cards – everyone has a good evening, although they are sorry to lose money to Grice. When it is time to go to sleep, Dirt Sheets puts the dead man's feet, still in the boots, behind the fire to thaw overnight.

In the morning, Dirt Sheets gets up early so that he can go and send birthday greetings to his mother by telegraph[10]. He takes the boots and socks from the dead man's feet and leaves the feet behind. When Grice wakes up, he finds the dead man's feet and jumps to the wrong conclusion…

9 warm up
10 a method of communicating by sending electric signals through wires or by radio waves

Pre-reading activities

Key vocabulary

This section will help you familiarize yourself with some of the more specific vocabulary used in the story. You may want to use it to help you before you start reading, or as a revision exercise after you have finished the story.

Describing cowboy life

The narrator uses a lot of specific and specialized terms to describe the lives of the cowboys in the story.

1 **Look at the 12 words and phrases in bold in the extracts below. Which refer to a) clothes b) equipment c) buildings or places?**

1 *They wore **blanket coats**, woolly **chaps**, **grease-wool scarves** tied over their hats and under their bristled chins, **sheepskin mitts**…*

2 *Too late to try for the **bunkhouse**. Old man Grice's **shack** is somewheres up along. He's bound a have…a hot **stove**.*

3 *We'll put our horses up. Where's the **barn**?*

4 *Barn. Never had one. There's a **lean-to** out there behind the **woodpile** should keep em from blowin away or maybe freezin.*

5 *Sheets pulled out a **Bowie knife** and sawed through Montana's shins just above the boot tops, put the booted feet in his **saddlebags**…*

2 **Match the words in bold in exercise 1 with their definitions (a–l) below.**

Clothes

a) warm jackets made from heavy wool, traditionally worn by the native people of North America in cold weather

b) pieces of cloth used for keeping your neck and head warm, treated so that water cannot get through

c) pieces of leather that cowboys wear over their trousers to protect their legs when riding horses

d) very warm gloves

Equipment

e) a hunting weapon commonly carried by cowboys

f) a kind of heater, in this case one that burns wood, used to keep a house or building warm

g) leather containers used for carrying things on horseback, usually worn over a horse's neck or back

Buildings or places

h) a large building on a farm or ranch where animals, crops or machinery are kept

i) a building where a group of workers sleep

j) a simple outdoor building that normally uses the side of another building as one of its walls

k) a very simple and basic building, in this case used as a home

l) a large pile of firewood stored outside, often near a house or farm

Adjectives

The author uses adjectives to describe both the cowboys and their surroundings.

3 **Look at the adjectives and their definitions below. Then choose an appropriate word from the list to complete the sentences below.**

> **bitter** extremely cold in a way which makes you very uncomfortable
> **savvy** knowing a lot about something and able to make good judgments about it
> **scorching** extremely hot, burning, painful
> **spirited** full of energy
> **vain** very proud, thinking you are attractive or special

1 As he opened the door, the man gasped as the .... cold hit his face.

2 The group was convinced after her .... defence of the proposal.

3 The desert was a lonely, cruel place, full of extremes – freezing by night, and .... by day.

4 She bought her laptop on the advice of her friend, who was very .... about computers.

5 When the man walked in, you could tell he thought highly of himself – he was so .... he couldn't help looking in every mirror he passed.

Non-standard language

Spelling

When the narrator reports the words of the characters, she often uses non-standard spelling to help her bring the cowboys' voices and conversations to life.

4 Look at the extracts below. Notice how the letters at the beginning or end of some words (such as 'th' or 'g') are dropped, and how words like *of* and *to* are substituted with *a*. Rewrite the extracts using standard spelling.

1 *I'll cut em off and thaw em after supper*

_____

2 *He's bound a have dried prunes*

_____

3 *A lean-to…should keep em from blowin away or maybe freezin*

_____

4 *Hot biscuits just comin out a the oven*

_____

Grammar

The cowboys' speech contains many examples of non-standard grammar.

5 Look at extracts 1–4 below and find examples of:

a) a double negative
b) a past simple form where there should be a past participle
c) an adjective where there should be an adverb

1 *He's ate Sheets.*
2 *Eat your bacon, don't make no trouble.*

3 *The arithmetic stood comfortable.*
4 *There's enough trouble in the world without no more.*

6 **Look again at the four extracts in exercise 5. Rewrite them using standard grammar.**

Picturesque descriptions

Both the narrator and the characters in the story often use interesting phrases to describe everyday things.

7 **Look at the extracts below. Match the phrases in bold with the more usual words and phrases in the box.**

---

alcohol   feet   lively horse   dead man   son's greeting   not so good

---

1 *Dirt Sheets…was all right on top but his luck was **running muddy** near the bottom, no socks and curl-toe boots cracked and holed.*
2 *"That **can a corn beef'**s wearing my size boots," Sheets said and got off his horse for the first time that day.*
3 *Pull up a chair and have some a this son-of-a-bitch stew. And I got plenty **conversation juice** a wash it down.*
4 *He…pulled the boots and socks off the originals, drew them on to his own **pedal extremities**.*
5 *It was his mother's birthday and if he wanted to telegraph a **filial sentiment** to her…*
6 *Sleep where you can find a space, but…don't bother that blood bay… He's a **spirited steed**.*

Main themes

Before you read the story, you may want to think about some of its main themes. The questions will help you think about the story as you are reading it for the first time. There is more discussion of the main themes in the *Literary analysis* section after the story.

Landscape

The vast plains of Wyoming with their wildness and extreme temperatures are potentially deadly environments, and this is the context in which the story takes place. Annie Proulx has spoken of her use of landscape as a starting point for all the stories that she writes. The scale of the landscape emphasizes the vulnerability[11] of the people who live there.

8 As you read the story, ask yourself:

a) What do we know about the environment in which old man Grice lives?

b) How do you think living alone in this landscape has affected old man Grice's character and view of life?

Life and death

Spending long periods of time in such a harsh environment – vulnerable to the weather, wild animals and other people, and far away from towns where they might get food or medical supplies – cowboys often see death as an 'occupational hazard', a risk of the job.

9 As you read the story, consider these questions:

a) What precautions do the cowboys take to help them survive in the harsh landscape?

b) What seems to be the attitude of the cowboys and old man Grice to each other? How is this shown?

11 the ease with which someone can be hurt physically or mentally

The Blood Bay

by Annie Proulx

The winter of 1886–87 was terrible. Every goddamn[12] history of the high plains says so. There were great stocks of cattle on **overgrazed** land during the droughty[13] summer. Early wet snow froze hard so the cattle could not break through the **crust** to the grass. Blizzards and freeze-eye cold followed, the gaunt bodies of cattle **piling up** in draws and coulees[14].

A young Montana cowboy, somewhat vain, had **skimped** on coat and **mittens** and put all his wages into a fine pair of handmade boots. He crossed into Wyoming Territory thinking it would be warmer, for it was south of where he was. That night he froze to death on Powder River's bitter west bank, that stream of famous dimensions and direction – an **inch** deep, a mile wide and she flows uphill from Texas.

The next afternoon three cowpunchers from the Box Spring outfit near Suggs rode past his corpse, blue as a whetstone[15] and half-buried in snow. They were savvy and salty[16]. They wore blanket coats, woolly chaps, grease-wool scarves tied over their hats and under their **bristled** chins, sheepskin mitts and two of them were fortunate enough to park their feet in good boots and heavy socks. The third, Dirt Sheets, a **cross-eyed** drinker of hair-oil, was all right on top but his luck was running muddy near the bottom, no socks and curl-toe boots cracked and holed.

"That can a corn beef's wearing my size boots," Sheets said and got off his horse for the first time that day. He pulled at the Montana cowboy's left boot but it was frozen on. The right one didn't come off any easier.

12 *US, slang:* used for emphasizing what you are saying, especially when you are angry or annoyed. Some people consider this word offensive
13 lacking rain
14 valleys or channels that water flows through
15 a stone on which you rub metal blades in order to make them sharper
16 *old-fashioned:* clever and funny

"Son of a sick steer in a snowbank," he said, "I'll cut em off and thaw em after supper." Sheets pulled out a Bowie knife and sawed through Montana's **shins** just above the boot tops, put the booted feet in his saddlebags, admiring the **tooled** leather and topstitched hearts and clubs. They rode on down the river looking for strays, found a dozen bogged in deep **drifts** and lost most of the daylight getting them out.

"Too late to try for the bunkhouse. Old man Grice's shack is somewheres up along. He's bound a have dried **prunes** or other **dainties** or at least a hot stove."

The temperature was dropping, so cold that **spit** crackled in the air and a man didn't dare to piss[17] for fear he'd be **rooted fast** until spring. They agreed it must be forty below[18] and more, the wind scything[19] up a nice Wyoming howler[20].

They found the shack four miles north. Old man Grice opened the door a **crack**.

"Come on in, puncher or **rustler**, I don't care."

"We'll put our horses up. Where's the barn?"

"Barn. Never had one. There's a lean-to out there behind the woodpile should keep em from blowin away or maybe freezin. I got my two horses in here beside the dish cupboard. I **pamper** them babies somethin terrible. Sleep where you can find a space, but I'm tellin you don't bother that blood bay none, he will mull you up and spit you out. He's a spirited steed. Pull up a chair and have some a this son-of-a-bitch stew. And I got plenty conversation juice a wash it down. Hot biscuits just comin out a the oven."

It was a fine evening, eating, drinking and playing cards, swapping lies, the stove kicking out heat, old man Grice's **spoiled** horses sighing in comfort. The only disagreeable tone to the evening from the waddies'[21] point of view was the fact that

17 *impolite*: to get rid of waste liquid from your body. A more polite word is pee or wee. The formal word is urinate
18 forty degrees below zero
19 *poetic*: a scythe is a tool used for cutting long grass or grain, consisting of a wooden handle and a long curved metal blade. Here it is used as a verb to describe the effect of the wind
20 *slang*: wind
21 US, *slang*: cowboy

their host cleaned them out[22], took them for three dollars and four bits[23]. Around midnight Grice blew out the lamp and got in his bunk and the three punchers stretched out on the floor. Sheets set his **trophies** behind the stove, laid his head on his **saddle** and went to sleep.

He woke half an hour before daylight, recalled it was his mother's birthday and if he wanted to telegraph a filial sentiment to her he would have to ride faster than chain lightning[24] with the links snapped, for the Overland office[25] closed at noon. He checked his **grisly** trophies, found them thawed and pulled the boots and socks off the originals, drew them on to his own pedal extremities. He threw the bare Montana feet and his old boots in the corner near the dish cupboard, slipped out like a falling feather, saddled his horse and rode away. The wind was low and the fine cold air refreshed him.

Old man Grice was up with the sun **grinding** coffee beans and frying bacon. He glanced down at his rolled-up guests and said, "Coffee's ready." The blood bay stamped and kicked at something that looked like a man's foot. Old man Grice took a closer look.

"There's a bad start to the day," he said, "it is a man's foot and there's the other." He counted the sleeping guests. There were only two of them.

"Wake up, survivors, for god's sake wake up and get up."

The two punchers rolled out, stared **wild-eyed** at the old man who was fairly[26] **frothing**, pointing at the feet on the floor behind the blood bay.

"He's ate Sheets. Ah, I knew he was a hard horse, but to eat a man whole. You **savage** bugger[27]," he screamed at the blood bay and drove him out into the scorching cold. "You'll never eat human meat again. You'll sleep out with the blizzards and

22 *slang*: beat them at cards
23 *US, old-fashioned*: an amount of money worth 12½ cents
24 *mainly US*: lightning that moves quickly in zigzag lines
25 the postal service at the time
26 *old-fashioned*: used for emphasizing that something happens or is done in an extreme way
27 *impolite*: an insulting word for someone who is stupid or annoying

wolves, you hell-bound fiend[28]." Secretly he was pleased to own a horse with the sand[29] to eat a **raw** cowboy.

The leftover Box Spring riders were up and drinking coffee. They **squinted** at old man Grice, **hitched** at their gun belts.

"Ah, boys, for god's sake, it was a terrible accident. I didn't know what a **brute** of a animal was that blood bay. Let's keep this to ourselves. Sheets was no prize and I've got forty gold dollars says so and the three and four bits I took off a you last night. Eat your bacon, don't make no trouble. There's enough trouble in the world without no more."

No, they wouldn't make trouble and they put the heavy money in their saddlebags, drank a last cup of hot coffee, saddled up and rode out into the grinning morning.

When they saw Sheets that night at the bunkhouse they nodded, congratulated him on his mother's birthday but said nothing about blood bays or forty-three dollars and four bits. The arithmetic stood comfortable.

28 *mainly literary*: a very evil person or monster
29 *slang*: courage

Post-reading activities

Understanding the story

Use these questions to help you check that you have understood the story.

1   What was so terrible about the winter of 1886–87?
2   Why did the Montana cowboy freeze to death?
3   Why do the dead man's boots appeal to Sheets so much?
4   What does Sheets have to do to get 'Montana's' boots off him?
5   Why do the men decide to go to old man Grice's?
6   Where do Grice's horses usually sleep?
7   Generally speaking, the men enjoy their evening at Grice's. What is the only thing they don't enjoy?
8   Where does Sheets put Montana's feet overnight? Why?
9   In the morning, what does Sheets do with the feet?
10 Why does he leave earlier than the others?
11 When old man Grice sees the feet, what does he think has happened?
12 How much does the old man give the Box Spring riders? Why?
13 What do they say to Sheets when they see him later? What don't they say?

Language study

Using *so*

The simple word *so* has many common uses in English. Here are three of the most common:
a) to add emphasis to an adjective, adverb or noun phrase
b) to link two clauses within a sentence, and show why someone or something does something
c) to refer back to something that has already been mentioned

1   Look at the extracts below and match the examples of *so* with their uses (a–c) above.

1   *The winter of 1886–87 was terrible. Every goddamn history of the high plains says **so**.*
2   *Early wet snow froze hard **so** the cattle could not break through the crust to the grass.*

3 *Sheets was no prize and I've got forty gold dollars says* **so**.
4 *The temperature was dropping,* **so** *cold that spit crackled in the air.*

2 Rewrite the sentences below, using *so* to make the two sentences into one.

1 At night, the cowboy was cold. He froze to death.

2 At the end of a day's work, the cowboys were tired. They would sleep like the dead.

3 Sheets loved his mother. He got up early to send her a telegram for her birthday.

4 The old man was worried that his horse had eaten Sheets. He gave the other cowboys money to keep quiet.

5 The cowboys knew that the horse hadn't eaten Sheets. They didn't say that the horse hadn't eaten him to old man Grice.

3 Rewrite each pair of sentences below as one sentence, using *so* and replacing or modifying the words in bold.

1 Dirt Sheets liked the boots **a lot**. He cut the man's feet off to get them.

2 The men worked **hard**. They were exhausted at the end of the day.

3 The cowboys feared the night cold **very much.** They slept on the floor of old man Grice's shack.

4 The horse bit people **often**. Old man Grice warned them to stay away from her.

Compound nouns and adjectives

A compound is a word which is formed from two or more other words, such as 'cow' + 'boy' = *cowboy*.

4 Match a word from box A with a word from box B to form ten new compounds.

A	bunk	day	hand	left	mid	saddle	sheep	snow	up	wood

B	bags	bank	hill	house	light	made	night	over	pile	skin

5 Look at the new compounds in exercise 4. Decide if each one is a) a noun or b) an adjective.

6 Use compounds from exercise 4 to complete the sentences below.

1 It was a long .... climb and we were exhausted when we got to the top.
2 He was wearing an enormous old .... coat that looked like it had never been washed.
3 It was a real shame to throw away all that .... food, so she put it in a bag and took it home.
4 The first dim rays of .... showed grey in the distance as they set off.
5 She was so touched by her granddaughter's special .... card that tears welled in her eyes.

7 Write five more sentences using the remaining compounds from exercise 4.

Literary analysis

Plot

1 Make a list of the main events in the story. Are they told in the order they happened? Is there one event which is more important than the others, or are they all equally important?
2 Are you interested in knowing what happens next, or do you think the story has come to a satisfying conclusion?

Character

3 How many characters are there in the story? What do we know about them?

4 What is the main difference between the young cowboy from Montana and the three cowboys who find his body? What does this tell us about the life of a cowboy at the time the story is set?

5 How do you react to Sheets taking the dead man's boots? Does it shock you? Why/Why not? Does it shock or surprise his friends? Why/Why not?

6 Think of three adjectives to describe old man Grice. Think of examples of his actions or words that justify your choices.

7 What is old man Grice's reaction to (wrongly) discovering that his horse has eaten Dirt Sheets? What does Dirt Sheets's death mean to old man Grice? What does this tell us about the men's attitude to life and death?

8 Think about all the characters who appear in the story, dead and alive, human and animal. Which character do you think is described most directly, and most fully? Why do you think that is?

9 Why do the other cowboys decide not to tell Sheets about the money they got from old man Grice? What does this tell us about the relationship between the cowboys? Do they trust each other? Why/Why not?

Narration

10 Does the narrator give us any direct information about the thoughts and feelings of the characters? What effect does this have?

11 The writer uses a lot of dialogue in the story. What does the dialogue tell us about the plot and the characters?

12 Read the opening sentences again. Notice how it sounds as though the text is being spoken out loud by a storyteller who uses the same colourful language as the characters:

The winter of 1886–87 was terrible. Every goddamn history of the high plains says so. There were great stocks of cattle on overgrazed land during the droughty summer. Early wet snow froze hard so the cattle could not break through the crust to the grass. Blizzards and freeze-eye cold followed, the gaunt bodies of cattle piling up in draws and coulees.

Who do you imagine the narrator to be? Why?

Style

13　The narrator often plays with words to create surprising and memorable images. Look at the example below. Notice how the writer uses the verb 'freeze' and the noun 'eye' to create a new adjective 'freeze-eye'. What kind of cold is *freeze-eye cold*? What sense is the writer appealing to? What effect does the adjective create?

Blizzards and freeze-eye cold followed.

14　Here are some more examples from the text. Look at the words and phrases in bold. What does each description mean? What effect does it create?

*his luck was **running muddy** near the bottom*
*no socks and **curl-toe** boots cracked and holed.*
*slipped out **like a falling feather***
*rode out into the **grinning** morning*

15　The story talks about the tragic death of a young man. Is the atmosphere of the story tragic? If not, what adjective would you use to describe the atmosphere? Do you think the story is teaching us a lesson, or just trying to amuse us?

Guidance to the above literary terms, answer keys to all the exercises and activities, plus a wealth of other reading-practice material, can be found at www.macmillanenglish.com/readers.

Essay questions

Language analysis

> Discuss how one of the language areas you have studied contributes to the telling of two of the stories in the collection.

Analysing the question

What is the question asking?

It is asking you to:
- choose one language area from the index on page 205
- explain how this language area functions in the context of storytelling
- use examples from two of the stories in the collection.

Preparing your answer

1 Look back through the *Language study* sections of the stories you've read and choose a language area that you feel confident about and that applies to the telling of two, or more, of the stories.
2 Make notes about the language area. Include notes on form, function and use.
3 Choose examples from two stories. Choose examples from both classic and contemporary stories, if possible.
4 Look back at the question and your notes and plan your essay. Here is an example of an essay plan:

Introduction	Introduce the area you are going to talk about.
Main body 1	Explain the general function of the area you have chosen; use examples from both stories.
Main body 2	Analyze how the area contributes to the style of both stories, referring to specific passages in the stories.
Conclusion	Summarize the literary use and function of the language area you focused on.

Literary analysis

> Choose two of the stories from the collection and comment on the relationship between the main characters. Compare and contrast the root of the tensions in their relationships.

Analysing the question

What is the question asking?

It is asking you to:
- look at two stories in the collection
- analyze the relationship between the main characters in the two stories
- identify and comment on the tensions in their relationships
- describe any differences and similarities between the relationships.

Preparing your answer

1 Choose two stories from the collection that you enjoyed and could relate to. Make notes about the relationship between the main characters in each story. Does the relationship change during the course of the story? Why/Why not?
2 Make notes on the tensions in the relationship. Think about what causes these tensions and the effect they have on the relationship. Have these tensions been resolved by the end of the story?
3 Choose passages from the two stories that show the tension and any significant changes in the relationship. Make a note of any useful quotations.
4 Make a list of the main similarities and differences between the relationships and the way they evolve.

5   Read the question again and write a plan for your essay. Here is an
    example:

Introduction	Briefly introduce the two stories and how they link to the main theme of the question (tensions in personal relationships).
Story 1	Describe and comment on the relationship in the first story.
Story 2	Describe and comment on the relationship in the second story.
Similarities	Discuss the similarities between the relationships in the two stories.
Differences	Discuss the differences between the relationships in the two stories.
Conclusion	Make a general comment about the theme of tensions in personal relationships in literature (or in this particular collection).

For tips on writing academic essays, and essays about literary analysis, visit the Macmillan Readers website at: www.macmillanenglish.com/readers.

Glossary

The definitions in the glossary refer to the meanings of the words and phrases as they are used in the short stories in this collection. Some words and phrases may also have other meanings which are not given here. The definitions are arranged in the story in which they appear, and in alphabetical order.

A Lesson on a Tortoise

anticipate (v) to be excited about something enjoyable that is going to happen soon

appeal (n) a request for people to do something or to behave in a particular way

covert (adj) secret

cripple (v) to make a part of someone's body very painful, especially when they walk

deferential (adj) showing that you respect someone and want to treat them politely

degradation (n) a situation or condition that makes someone feel ashamed and makes people lose respect for them

distress (n) a feeling that you have when you are very unhappy, worried or upset

divulge (v) *formal:* to give information about something, especially something that should be kept secret

droop (v) to hang downwards

earnest (adj) serious, determined and meaning what you say

ecstasy (n) a feeling of great happiness and pleasure

erratic (adj) changing often or not following a regular pattern, so that it is difficult to know what will happen next

flush (v) if someone flushes, their face becomes red because they are hot or ill, or are feeling angry, embarrassed or excited

furtive (adj) done quickly and secretly to avoid being noticed

glare (v) to look at someone or something in a very angry way

hobble (v) to walk slowly and with difficulty because your feet are sore or injured

hymn (n) a religious song that people usually sing in churches

impudent (adj) behaving in a rude way that shows no respect for someone

insolent (adj) rude, especially when you should be showing respect

intrude (v) to enter a place where you are not allowed to go

lacquer (n) a liquid that you put onto the surface of wood or metal to make it shiny

lad (n) *British, informal:* a boy or a young man

limp (adj) not firm, stiff or strong

novelty (n) the excitement or interest that something new or unusual creates

nudge (v) to use a part of your body, especially your elbow, to give a little push to someone or something

pack (n) a group of animals that hunt together

plaintive (adj) high and sad

saw (v) to cut something with a saw, a tool with a handle and a metal blade with several sharp teeth along one edge

scorn (n) a feeling that someone or something is not good enough to deserve your approval or respect

scrap (n) a small piece of something such as paper or cloth

shifty (adj) *informal:* looking dishonest

skulk (v) to move around or to wait somewhere in a secret way, especially because you are going to do something bad

slack (adj) not taking enough care to make sure that something is done well

smear (v) to make the surface of something dirty by rubbing it

sneak (n) a person who tells someone in authority about something wrong that you have done; this word shows that you dislike people who do this

sordid (adj) dirty and ugly

spring (v) to jump or move in a particular direction, quickly and with a lot of energy

stock (n) an amount of something that you keep so that you can use it when you need it

stride (n) a long step

strip (n) a piece of something that is much longer than it is wide

twig (n) a very small thin branch from a tree or bush

uneasy (adj) slightly nervous, worried or upset about something

weariness (n) something that makes you feel very tired

well-to-do (adj) rich and belonging to an upper-class family

wretched (adj) *informal:* used for emphasizing how much someone or something annoys you

yield (v) to finally agree to do what someone else wants you to do

The Teddy-bears' Picnic

before you can blink PHRASE very quickly

bent (adj) a curved or twisted shape

bewildered (adj) confused and not certain what to do

bouncy (adj) happy, lively and enthusiastic

carburettor (n) the part of an engine, that mixes air and petrol in order to provide power

castor (n) one of a set of small wheels that can move in any direction and are often attached to the bottom of a piece of furniture or equipment

chap (n) *British, informal, old-fashioned:* a man, especially one that you like

clutch (v) to hold someone or something firmly, for example because you are afraid or in pain, or do not want to lose them

couch (v) *formal:* express

cry out to do something PHRASAL VERB to really need to do something

decanter (n) a special glass bottle that you pour an alcoholic drink into before serving it to people

dismantle (v) to separate the parts of something such as a machine so that they no longer form a single unit

dozy (adj) tired and likely to go to sleep

drag along PHRASAL VERB to make someone go to a place when they do not want to

dress up PHRASAL VERB to put on clothes that make you look like someone else, for fun

drift (v) to go from one state to another without realizing it

dumpy (adj) *informal:* short and fat

dwell on PHRASAL VERB to spend a lot of time thinking or talking about something unpleasant

engagement (n) the period during which two people have agreed to get married

excruciating (adj) used for emphasizing how bad something is

fiddle at PHRASAL VERB to touch or move something with many small quick movements of your fingers because you are bored, nervous or concentrating on something else

floppy (adj) soft and hanging down in a loose or heavy way

flourish (adj) a confident movement made so that other people notice

frown (v) to move your eyebrows down and closer together because you are annoyed, worried or thinking hard

fuss (n) a lot of unnecessary worry or excitement about something

fussy (adj) containing too many small parts or details

get into a state PHRASE *informal:* to become very nervous or worried

gibe (n) a remark that is intended to hurt someone or to make them feel stupid

gooey (adj) *informal:* showing feelings such as love or admiration in a silly way

grotesque (adj) unreasonable or offensive

gurgle (n) a low sound in the throat

half-wit (n) *informal:* someone who is stupid or who has done something stupid

ignition (n) the part of a car's engine that makes the fuel start to burn so that the car can start

in bloom PHRASE if a tree or plant is in bloom, it is covered with flowers

jolly (adj) *old-fashioned:* lively and enjoyable

let down PHRASAL VERB to make someone disappointed by not doing something that they are expecting you to do

lilt (v) a pleasant rising and falling pattern of sounds in the way that someone talks or in a piece of music

loft (n) a space under the roof of a building, often used for storing things

odd (adj) unusual or unexpected in a way that attracts your interest or attention

overlook (v) to fail to notice or consider someone

parapet (n) a low wall at the edge of something high such as a bridge or a roof

patronize (v) to behave or talk in a way that shows you think you are more intelligent or important than someone else

peer (v) to look very carefully, especially because something is difficult to see

pompous (adj) someone who is pompous thinks they are very important and speaks or behaves in a very serious and formal way

proceedings (n) an event or series of related events

prod (v) to push someone or something quickly with your finger, or with an object that has a long thin end

protrude (v) to be further forward than the rest of something

put something down to PHRASAL VERB if you put something down to a particular reason, you think it has happened for that reason

quarrel (n) an argument, especially one about something unimportant between people who know each other well

repulsive (adj) someone or something that is repulsive is so unpleasant that you feel slightly ill when you see them or think about them

reservation (n) a feeling of doubt about whether something is good or right

root around PHRASAL VERB to search for something by putting your hand deep into a place and pushing things around

scratch (n) a cut on the surface of your skin

scrawny (adj) very thin, in a way that is not attractive or healthy

screech (v) to make a loud, high and unpleasant noise

screw up your features PHRASE to pull your forehead down and push your mouth and nose up, usually to show that you dislike something

self-deprecating (adj) showing that you think you are not very good or important

shoot up PHRASAL VERB to grow taller very quickly

siphon (n) a tube used for moving liquid from one container to another

skewer (n) a long thin piece of metal or wood that you stick through food to hold it while it cooks

snap (v) to speak to someone in a sudden, angry way

snout (n) the long nose of a pig or a similar animal

sound (adj) satisfactory, healthy

speculation (n) attempts to make a large profit by buying and selling things such as property or shares

splay (v) to stretch or spread something, especially your body or part of your body, in a way that often looks strange

split your sides PHRASE *informal:* to laugh a lot

squash (n) *British:* a sweet drink made from fruit juice, sugar and water

squat (v) to bend your knees and lower yourself towards the ground so that you balance on your feet

squirt (n) a small amount of liquid moved with a lot of force

stout (adj) slightly fat; this word is less rude than 'fat'

strain (n) pressure caused by a difficult situation

stumble (v) to move with difficulty and nearly fall because you are tired or ill

tacit (adj) expressed or understood without being said directly

tartan (adj) a pattern of colourful lines and squares on cloth that is typical of Scotland

telltale (adj) telltale signs of something are obvious signs that it exists or it has happened

the shakes (n) *informal:* uncontrolled quick movements of your body that you make because, for example, you are ill, nervous or have drunk too much alcohol

tightrope (n) a piece of rope or wire high above the ground that a performer walks along in a circus

tiresome (adj) making you feel annoyed or bored

topple (v) to stop being steady and fall

totter (v) to stand or move in a way that is not steady

trifle (n) a sweet food eaten especially in the UK, made from cake covered with fruit or jelly, cold custard and sometimes cream

twitch (n) a sudden slight uncontrolled movement of your body

vow (v) *formal:* to promise that you will do something

wind up PHRASAL VERB if you wind up an object, you make it operate by turning a part of it around and around

The Rough Crossing

abreast (adv) next to each other, facing or moving in the same direction

abroad (adj) *old-fashioned:* away from your home

abstracted (adj) *formal:* thinking about something so much that you do not seem to notice the world around you

accomplish (v) to succeed in doing something

array (n) a large group of people or things that are related in some way

ashore (adv) to or onto land from the water or a ship

assembly (n) a group of people who meet together for a particular reason

atone (v) *formal:* to show that you are sorry for doing something bad or wrong

awed (adj) feeling great respect, admiration and sometimes fear for something

be endowed with something PHRASE to have something such as a good ability or quality

befuddled (adj) very confused, and unable to think clearly

bind (v) to limit what someone is allowed to do by making them obey a rule or agreement

blatant (adj) very obvious

boom (n) a long pole attached to the bottom of a boat's sail, that is used for changing the direction of the sail

bow (v) to bend your body forwards from the waist, especially to show respect for someone

breach (n) a failure to follow a law or rule

bruise (v) to cause a mark to appear on someone's body by hitting or knocking it

brunette (n) a woman with dark brown hair

bundle (n) something that is wrapped in something soft such as a blanket so that you cannot see its real shape

burden (n) *literary*: something heavy that you have to carry

butt in PHRASAL VERB *informal*: to join a conversation or activity without being asked to

calamity (n) an event that causes serious damage, or causes a lot of people to suffer, for example a flood or fire

chaperone (v) to go somewhere with a young woman or group of children to make sure that they behave well

cling (v) to hold onto someone or something tightly with your hands or arms

curt (adj) using few words in a way that shows you are impatient or angry

customs (n) the place at a port, airport or border where officials check that the goods that people are bringing into a country are legal, and whether they should pay customs duties

defer to PHRASAL VERB *formal*: to accept someone's opinion or decision, especially because you respect them

deft (adj) moving quickly and with skill

deliver yourself of PHRASAL VERB *formal*: to make or produce something

diffidence (n) shyness

drench (v) to make someone or something very wet

drown out PHRASAL VERB to prevent a sound from being heard by making a louder noise

dwindle (v) to become gradually less or smaller over a period of time until almost nothing remains

elude (v) *formal*: if a fact, idea, or word eludes you, you cannot remember or understand it

fancy dress (n) *British*: clothes that you wear for fun to make you look like a particular famous person or a particular type of person, at a fancy-dress party

fiancé (n) your fiancé is the man you are engaged to and are going to get married to

flight (n) a set of stairs going from one level to another

fling (v) to throw something carelessly or with a lot of force

gleam (v) to shine brightly

glib (adj) a glib person speaks easily and confidently; this word shows that you do not trust the person or what they are saying

gong (n) a large circular metal object hanging from a frame; you hit it to make a loud deep noise

grief (n) a strong feeling of sadness, usually because someone has died

hearty (adj) friendly and enthusiastic, sometimes in a slightly annoying way

high-handed (adj) speaking or acting without considering other people's opinions

hysterical (adj) behaving in an uncontrolled way because you are extremely excited, afraid or upset

imprudent (adj) *formal:* not sensible

incrustation (n) a layer of material which forms slowly on something

innuendo (n) the use of statements with a second possible meaning, usually referring to sex and intended as a joke

jostle (v) to push against someone because you are trying to move past them in a crowd

languid (adj) *literary:* someone who is languid is weak or ill

lash (v) to tie something firmly to something else, or to tie two things together firmly using a rope

lethargy (n) the feeling of lacking energy and not wanting to do anything

linger (v) to stay somewhere longer than is necessary, or to spend longer doing something than is necessary, because it is enjoyable or helpful to you

listless (adj) feeling as if you have no energy and no interest in anything

lunge (v) to move suddenly and with a lot of force in order to catch, hit or avoid something or someone

makeshift (adj) made using whatever is available and therefore not very good

morose (adj) feeling unhappy, in a bad mood, and not wanting to talk to anyone

nap (n) a short sleep, usually during the day

oblique (adj) not looking or pointing directly at someone or something

outrage (n) an event or action that makes you feel extremely angry and upset

overwhelm (v) to surprise someone very much

porcelain (n) a hard shiny white substance used for making expensive dishes, cups, decorations, etc

portentous (adj) *formal:* giving a warning about the future

precipitate (adj) *formal:* done too quickly, and without enough thought or preparation

quarters (n) *formal:* rooms or buildings for people to live in

rasp (v) to make an unpleasant sound as if two rough surfaces were rubbing together, especially when speaking or breathing

rehearsal (n) an occasion when you practise for the performance of a play, concert, opera, etc

roll-top (n) a curved cover that you can pull down and lock

sanguine (adj) *formal:* confident and hopeful about what might happen, especially in a difficult situation

sardonic (adj) showing a lack of respect for what someone else has said or done

scant (adj) very little, or not enough

shiver (n) a shaking movement that your body makes when you are cold, frightened or excited

show off PHRASAL VERB to behave in a way that is intended to attract people's attention and make them admire you

slick (adj) smooth and shiny

slip (v) if you slip, your feet slide accidentally and you lose your balance or fall over

slouch (v) to sit, walk or stand with your shoulders bent forwards and your head low so that you look lazy

slump (v) to be in a position that is not upright

soak (v) to make something very wet, or to become very wet

solicitous (adj) *formal:* behaving in a way that shows you care about someone's health, feelings, safety, etc

split (v) to share something by dividing it into separate parts

staccato (adj) in music, staccato notes are played or sung so that each note is clearly separate

start (n) a sudden movement that you make because you are surprised or afraid

startle (v) to make a person or animal feel suddenly frightened or surprised by doing something that they do not expect

sullen (adj) showing that you are in an unhappy mood, and do not want to talk

swamp (v) to fill or cover something with water

tender (adj) gentle in a way that shows that you care about someone or something

the elements (n) the weather, especially wind and rain

throng (v) if people throng somewhere, a lot of them go there

thrust (v) to move somewhere by pushing hard and quickly

timber (n) a piece of wood used for building

to and fro (adv) in one direction and then back again

transcend (v) *formal*: to go beyond

transverse (adj) placed sideways or at an angle across something

trite (adj) dull, unoriginal

tuck (n) a fold in clothing that you sew for decoration or to make the clothing tighter

utter (adj) complete; often used for emphasizing how bad someone or something is

vain (adj) unsuccessful, or useless

vault (n) a curved structure that supports or forms a roof

wan (adj) someone who is wan looks very pale and weak because they are ill

want (n) *formal*: a lack of something

whir (v) to make a fast repeated quiet sound

Lamb to the Slaughter

a trifle (n) *formal*: slightly

air (n) a feeling or attitude that someone has

alight (adj) *mainly literary*: bright, shining or burning

all of a sudden PHRASE very suddenly

amber (adj) between brown and yellow in colour

beg (v) to ask for help, an opportunity, etc in a way that shows you want it very much

belch (v) to let air from your stomach come out through your mouth in a noisy way

blunt instrument (n) any heavy object with a flat or round end, used as a weapon

cheesecake (n) a type of cake made of biscuits, soft cheese and sometimes fruit

chink (n) a very small space in a wall or between two things, especially when this lets light through

chop (n) a small piece of meat with a bone in it, usually from a sheep or a pig

clink (v) to make the short high sound of glass or metal objects hitting each other, or to cause objects to make this sound

cock (v) to raise or turn a part of your body

congeal (v) if a substance such as blood or fat congeals, it becomes thick and almost solid

console (v) to try to make someone feel better when they are unhappy or disappointed

cracker (n) a type of thin dry hard biscuit often eaten with cheese

cry your heart out PHRASE *informal*: to cry in an uncontrolled way

deep freeze (n) a freezer

draw (v) to pull something across a space in order to close or open it

go about your business PHRASE to do the things that you normally do

hospitality (n) friendly and generous behaviour towards visitors and guests, intended to make them feel welcome

hum (v) to make musical sounds with your lips closed

intent (adj) concentrating hard on something

longing (n) a strong feeling of wanting someone or something

loosely (adv) not firmly or tightly

luxuriate (v) to enjoy being in a very pleasant, comfortable, or relaxing situation or place

motionless (adj) not moving at all

nausea (n) the feeling that you are going to vomit

nip (n) a small amount of a strong alcoholic drink

pace (n) a step that you take when you walk or run

parcel (n) something wrapped in paper or in a large envelope

put up PHRASAL VERB to let someone stay in your house

shove (v) *informal:* to move something, or to put it somewhere, quickly and carelessly

sip (v) to drink in small amounts

slam (v) to close quickly with a loud noise

sloppy (adj) loose, untidy

swirl (n) a mass of something that moves in a twisting or circular motion

tinkle (v) to make a high ringing sound, or to make something ring with a high sound

touch up PHRASAL VERB to make your make-up look better by adding a little more

translucent (adj) a translucent colour is very pale or light

under your very nose PHRASE if something happens under your nose, it happens in a place or situation where you should notice it, but you do not

well up PHRASAL VERB if feelings well or well up inside you, they become very strong

yard (n) a unit for measuring length; there are three feet or 36 inches in a yard, and one yard is equal to 0.91 metres

The Rich Brother

appalled (adj) offended or shocked very much by something, because it is extremely unpleasant or bad

bandanna / bandana (n) a piece of coloured cloth worn around your head or neck

bead (n) a small drop of a liquid such as blood or sweat

blazer (n) a type of light jacket that is often worn as part of a uniform, for example by schoolchildren or members of a sports club

blessing (n) something good that you feel very grateful or lucky to have

blink (v) if a light blinks, it goes on and off continuously

blow (v) to destroy your own chance of succeeding, or to waste a good opportunity

brush off PHRASAL VERB to send someone away or refuse to listen to them

brutal (adj) extremely violent

burp (v) to make a noise when air from your stomach passes out through your mouth

casserole (n) food prepared in a deep dish with a lid, and cooked in the oven

catch on PHRASAL VERB to understand

cluster (n) a small group of people or things that are very close to each other

compulsion (n) a very strong feeling of wanting to do something, especially a feeling that you cannot control

concurrent (adj) *formal:* happening or done at the same time

creep (n) *informal:* an unpleasant person

crest (n) a design used as the symbol of a town, institution or family of high social class

debt (n) a situation in which you owe money to other people

ditch (n) a long narrow hole dug along the side of a road or field, usually so that water can run into it

due (adj) expected of someone

duffel bag (n) a large bag made from strong cloth that has a circular bottom and is pulled together at the top with a string

ember (n) the ash that is hot and red at the end of a cigar

expose (v) to fail to protect someone or something from something harmful or dangerous

find (n) something good, interesting or valuable that you discover by chance

fist (n) your hand when your fingers are closed tightly

foam over PHRASAL VERB if a fizzy drink is shaken or moved quickly, it might foam over – white bubbles go over the edges of the container that is holding it

for good PHRASE permanently, without the possibility of change in the future

franchise (n) a formal agreement for someone to sell a company's products or services in a particular place, in exchange for a payment or part of the profits

get your feet on the ground PHRASE to start feeling happy and confident in a new situation or place

grin (v) to smile showing your teeth

hang up PHRASAL VERB to stop using a telephone at the end of a conversation

hitchhike (v) to travel by asking other people to take you in their car, by standing at the side of a road and holding out your thumb or a sign

hollow (n) a small area in the ground that is lower than the ground around it

honk (v) to make a loud noise using a horn, especially the horn of a car

hood (n) the part of a coat or jacket that covers your head

hunch (v) to sit or stand with your back and shoulders curved forwards

in tongues PHRASE in strange languages that no one understands, usually due to extreme religious excitement

incarnation (n) the form or character that a person or thing takes at a particular time

inquisitor (n) someone who asks a long series of difficult questions in a very determined way in order to get information

intestine (n) the long tube in your body that processes food and carries waste out of your body

keep your own counsel PHRASE to say nothing about your plans or opinions

kid yourself PHRASE *informal:* to make yourself believe something that is not true

lay someone to rest PHRASE to bury someone's body in a ceremony after they have died

leg (n) a part of a journey

life sentence (n) a punishment in which someone is sent to prison for the rest of their life

loom (v) to appear as a large shape that is not clear, usually in a threatening way

musty (adj) smelling unpleasant and not fresh

particulars (n) information and details about someone or something

pitch (n) the things that you say to persuade someone to buy something or to support you

plaster (v) to cover a surface or a place with labels, advertisements, pictures, etc

play dumb PHRASE *informal:* to pretend to not know or not understand something

pop (n) *informal:* a sweet drink containing many bubbles

prophecy (n) a statement made by someone about something that they believe will happen

pucker (v) become full of folds or lines, and not flat

puff (n) the action of breathing in smoke from a cigarette, pipe, etc

quit (v) *informal:* to leave a place such as a job or a school permanently

real estate (n) *mainly US:* the business of buying and selling land and property

ring a bell PHRASE *informal:* something that rings a bell sounds familiar to you, although you cannot remember the exact details

ruddy (adj) red and looking healthy

rummage (v) to search for something among a lot of other things

scrutiny (n) careful examination of someone or something

service station (n) a business that sells petrol, oil and other things for vehicles

shallow (adj) taking in only a little air

shrug (v) to move your shoulders up and let them drop to show that you do not know something or do not care

skull (n) the bones of the head

skydiving (n) the sport of jumping out of a plane and falling for as long as possible before opening your parachute

sour (adj) unpleasant, unfriendly, or in a bad mood

specifics (n) the details of something

stale (adj) not fresh, no longer interested

stitch (n) a short piece of thread that is used for joining someone's skin together after it has been cut

stubble (n) the ends of plants that are left above ground after a farmer cuts a crop such as wheat or barley

stunt (n) something dangerous, for example jumping from a building, that is done to entertain people

telegram (n) a message that you send by telegraph, used especially in the past for short urgent messages

the bulk of PHRASE the majority or largest part of something

the gory details PHRASE *humorous:* the details about something that has happened, especially something unpleasant

tons (adv) *informal:* a lot

tumble (v) fall or roll along the ground

undiagnosed (adj) not having been identified, eg an illness

wasting (adj) a wasting disease makes you thin, weak and tired

when your ship comes in PHRASE *spoken:* used for talking about a time when you will have good luck

wreck (n) *informal:* someone who looks or feels very ill or tired

wrinkle (n) *informal:* a small problem

The Blood Bay

bristled (adj) covered with short stiff hairs

brute (n) a big strong animal, often that you do not like or that frightens you

crack (n) a narrow opening between two things or parts of things

cross-eyed (adj) having eyes that look towards each other slightly

crust (n) a hard layer of a substance covering a softer substance or a liquid

dainty (n) a special or delicious type of food

drift (n) a large pile of snow or sand formed by the wind

fast (adv) firmly and strongly or tightly

froth (v) *informal:* to be very annoyed, upset or excited about something

grind (v) to break something into very small pieces or powder, by using a machine or by crushing it between two hard surfaces

grisly (adj) involving death or violence in a shocking way

hitch (v) to move a part of your body or something that you are carrying to a higher position

inch (n) a unit for measuring length; an inch is equal to 2.54 centimetres, and there are 12 inches in one foot

mitten (n) a type of glove with one part for your thumb and another part for your fingers

overgrazed (adj) overgrazed land is damaged due to too many animals feeding on its grass

pamper (v) to look after someone or something very well, especially by making them feel very comfortable or by giving them nice things

pile up PHRASAL VERB to increase in number, often gathered one on top of another

prune (n) a dried plum

raw (adj) not cooked

rooted (adj) frozen, stuck

rustler (n) someone who steals farm animals such as sheep, cows or horses

saddle (n) a leather seat that you put on a horse's back when you ride it

savage (adj) cruel and unpleasant or violent

shin (n) the lower front part of your leg, between your knee and your ankle

skimp (v) to not use or provide enough of something

spit (n) *informal:* the clear liquid in your mouth

spoil (v) to treat someone with a lot of care and kindness

squint (v) to close your eyes slightly and try to see something, either because of a bright light or because your eyes do not work very well

tooled (adj) tooled leather has been decorated by pressing a design onto it using a special tool

trophy (n) something that you keep as proof of an achievement that you are proud of, for example a part of an animal that you have killed

wild-eyed (adj) someone who is wild-eyed looks very angry or frightened

Dictionary extracts adapted from the Macmillan English Dictionary © Macmillan Publishers Limited 2002

Language study index

Visit the Macmillan Readers website at
www.macmillanenglish.com/readers

to find FREE resources for use in class and for independent learning. Search our online catalogue to buy new Readers including audio download and eBook versions.

Here's a taste of what's available:

For the classroom:

- **Tests** for every Reader to check understanding and monitor progress
- **Worksheets** for every Reader to explore language and themes
- **Listening worksheets** to practise extensive listening
- Worksheets to help prepare for the **FCE reading exam**

Additional resources for students and independent learners:

- An **online level test** to identify reading level
- **Author information sheets** to provide in-depth biographical information about our Readers authors
- **Self-study worksheets** to help track and record your reading which can be used with any Reader
- Use our **creative writing worksheets** to help you write short stories, poetry and biographies
- Write academic essays and literary criticism confidently with the help of our **academic writing worksheets**
- Have fun completing our **webquests** and **projects** and learn more about the Reader you are studying
- Go backstage and read **interviews** with **famous authors** and **actors**
- Discuss your favourite Readers at the **Book Corner Club**

Visit www.macmillanenglish.com/readers to find out more!